A Guide to
STUDY SKILLS
and CAREERS in
CRIMINAL
JUSTICE and
PUBLIC
SECURITY

A Guide to

STUDY SKILLS
and CAREERS in
CRIMINAL
JUSTICE and
PUBLIC
SECURITY

Frank Schmalleger
University of North Carolina, Pembroke

Catherine D. Marcum
Appalachian State University

Los Angeles | London | New Delhi
Singapore | Washington DC | Melbourne

FOR INFORMATION:

SAGE Publications, Inc.
2455 Teller Road
Thousand Oaks, California 91320
E-mail: order@sagepub.com

SAGE Publications Ltd.
1 Oliver's Yard
55 City Road
London EC1Y 1SP
United Kingdom

SAGE Publications India Pvt. Ltd.
B 1/I 1 Mohan Cooperative Industrial Area
Mathura Road, New Delhi 110 044
India

SAGE Publications Asia-Pacific Pte. Ltd.
3 Church Street
#10-04 Samsung Hub
Singapore 049483

Printed in the United States of America

Library of Congress Cataloging-in-Publication Data

Names: Schmalleger, Frank, author. | Marcum, Catherine Davis, 1980- author.

Title: A guide to study skills and careers in criminal justice and public security/Frank Schmalleger, Catherine D. Marcum.

Description: Thousand Oaks : Sage, [2017] | Includes index.

Identifiers: LCCN 2015042931 | ISBN 978-1-5063-2370-1 (pbk.: alk. paper)

Subjects: LCSH: Criminal justice, Administration of—Vocational guidance—United States. | Criminal justice, Administration of—Study and teaching—United States. | Law enforcement—Vocational guidance—United States. | Law enforcement—Study and teaching—United States.

Classification: LCC HV9950 .S3533 2017 | DDC 364.973023—dc23 LC record available at http://lccn.loc.gov/2015042931

This book is printed on acid-free paper.

Acquisitions Editor: Jerry Westby
Editorial Assistant: Laura Kirkhuff
Production Editor: Veronica Stapleton Hooper
Copy Editor: Colleen B. Brennan
Typesetter: C&M Digitals (P) Ltd.
Proofreader: Tricia Currie-Knight
Indexer: Sheila Bodell
Cover Designer: Candice Harman
Illustrator: Sarah Yeh
Marketing Manager: Nicole Mangona

SFI Certified Sourcing
www.sfiprogram.org
SFI-00453

16 17 18 19 20 10 9 8 7 6 5 4 3 2 1

Brief Contents _____

Detailed Contents _____

Preface _____

A common complaint among criminal justice faculty is that many students are unaware of how to study effectively and how to successfully find employment in the criminal justice field after graduation. Students are unsure of how to (1) take helpful notes in class or while reading, (2) study effectively, (3) manage their time in an optimal manner, (4) write clearly and communicate well, (5) choose appropriate classes, (6) make the important transition from high school to college, and (7) find a job in their chosen field. Not only are students often unable to smoothly manage the higher education experience and all that it entails, but they are also unsure of the employment opportunities available to them. Pursuing a degree in criminal justice, for example, does not automatically mean that a person will become a law enforcement officer, although that is a common misperception in the field. There are many job options available to students who hold an associate's or bachelor's degree in criminal justice.

This text provides a how-to guide for student success in the study of criminal justice and in the pursuit of related degrees. It introduces the field of criminal justice and its subcomponents and also explains the employment opportunities available to criminal justice graduates. Its purpose is to help students better understand the discipline that they are about to enter. The text also provides instruction relevant to the seven points identified earlier, meaning that it will teach students how to effectively approach the study of criminal justice; communicate successfully with professors, peers, and potential employers; choose classes that will assist with career goals; make smart life choices while pursuing a college degree; develop good study skills; manage available time effectively; employ quality note taking; think creatively (i.e., develop thinking skills); and write purposefully and effectively within the discipline.

_____ **Acknowledgments**

Thank you to Jerry Westby, Laura Kirkhuff, and the staff at SAGE Publications for their assistance and patience with the preparation of this manuscript. It was wonderful to work with a group of individuals who shared the same vision for this book. We hope it brings our readers great success.

In addition, thank you to our talented illustrator Sarah Yeh for helping us fulfill our vision for the book.

Finally, thank you to all of the reviewers who provided invaluable feedback during the development of the book:

James W. Beeks, University of Phoenix and Kennesaw State University

Dianne Berger-Hill, Webster University

Terry Campbell, Kaplan University

Kevin Cannon, Southern Illinois University Edwardsville

Chris Chaney, William Jessup University

Veronyka James, Virginia Union University

Coy Johnston, Arizona State University

Shana L. Maier, Widener University

Eric Metchik, Salem State University

Jacqueline M. Mullany, Triton College

Jennifer Riggs, Eastern New Mexico University

Holli Vah Seliskar, Kaplan University

SaRita Stewart, Cedar Valley College

Katie L. Swope, Stevenson University

Amie Taylor, University of Phoenix

Angela Taylor, Fayetteville State University

Arnold R. Waggoner, Rose State College

Andrew Walker, West Virginia University at Parkersburg

Franzi Walsh, University of Phoenix

Andrew Wierenga, University of Phoenix

Thomas H. Williams, Community College of Denver

Denise R. Womer, Kaplan University

Tracey Woodard, University of North Florida

About the Authors _____

Frank Schmalleger, Ph.D., is distinguished professor emeritus at the University of North Carolina at Pembroke. He holds an undergraduate degree from the University of Notre Dame and both master's and doctoral degrees, with special emphasis in sociology, from The Ohio State University. From 1976 to 1994, he taught criminology and criminal justice courses at the University of North Carolina at Pembroke; for the last 16 of those years, he chaired the university's Department of Sociology, Social Work, and Criminal Justice. The university named him distinguished professor in 1991. Dr. Schmalleger is the author of numerous articles and more than 30 books, including the widely used *Criminal Justice Today* (Pearson, 2016), *Criminal Justice: A Brief Introduction* (Pearson, 2015), *Criminology Today* (Pearson, 2016), *Criminology: A Brief Introduction* (Pearson, 2015), and *Criminal Law Today* (Pearson, 2016).

Catherine D. Marcum, Ph.D., is associate professor of criminal justice at Appalachian State University and the criminal justice curriculum coordinator. She graduated with a Ph.D. in criminology from Indiana University of Pennsylvania in 2008. Since that time, she has published more than 40 peer-reviewed journal articles, written and edited multiple books, and been extremely active in the discipline on university, regional, and national levels. She was recently awarded Outstanding Educator of the Year by the Southern Criminal Justice Association. Her experience as a student and faculty member has given her insight into the needs and expectations of students and, more importantly, the common misperceptions of the field by students studying criminal justice.

Schmalleger: To all criminal justice, criminology, and security students—past, present, and future.
Marcum: I dedicate this book to my husband, Jeff, and my children, Drew and Maddy.

1

Criminal Justice and Public Safety

Congratulations! You have chosen a major that will lead to numerous opportunities for a wide variety of careers. In order to work effectively, the criminal justice system requires the efforts of tens of thousands of employees. In this chapter, we explore the three components of the criminal justice system, explain how they work together to enforce and apply the law, and, most importantly, discuss the various career opportunities available to you. Even though you are aware you want to get a job in the field of criminal justice, many of you are unsure of what type of criminal justice career to pursue. This chapter provides a multitude of information on the types of career opportunities available, but it may also be beneficial to take a personality test to see where you are best suited (e.g., Jung Typology Test). As you review this material, consider if you feel if it is a good fit for you.

American Criminal Justice System

The criminal justice system is composed of three components: police, criminal courts, and correctional agencies. According to the consensus perspective, these three agencies work together to ensure a smooth and fair processing of each offender through the criminal justice system in order to achieve a fair, just, and equitable outcome for all. Some argue, however, that the consensus perspective is overly idealistic and that justice agencies often have their own goals that conflict with one another. In

Facing the Court

addition, the constant competition for resources (e.g., programs, training, funding) makes it difficult for all stakeholders to work together without conflict on a consistent basis. Despite these opposing viewpoints, all three components are reliant on each other for successful processing of criminal suspects and convicted offenders. Figure 1.1 lists the broad categories of employment available in the criminal justice system, with more specific details provided in the sections that follow.

Figure 1-1 Criminal Justice System Employment Categories	
Attorney	Juvenile Court Officer
Bailiff	Local Law Enforcement
Clerk of the Court	Parole Officer
Corrections Officer	Probation Officer
Court Reporter	Security Officer
Crime Scene Investigator	Sheriff
Federal Law Enforcement	State Law Enforcement Officer
Judge	Victim's Advocate

Police

Police officers in the United States are charged with many responsibilities. Most importantly, they must uphold the law in a fair and just way, ensuring that the community is safe for its residents. The police mission is as follows: (1) enforce the law, (2) apprehend offenders, (3) prevent crime,

(4) ensure peace in the community, and (5) provide enforcement-related services. Although the media portray the role of law enforcement as an action-packed job involving constant high-speed chases, shoot-outs, and the breaking down of doors, only a small portion of the job involves answering calls that require such dramatic action. In fact, the majority of police work involves public service calls regarding quality-of-life offenses (e.g., noise complaints, vandalism, trespassing). These calls for service require the police to focus primarily on maintaining public order.

In order to achieve the missions listed in the previous paragraph, the police utilize core operational strategies. Preventative patrol, the backbone of police work since its inception, involves monitoring neighborhoods and communities (including virtual ones) using multiple techniques, such as traditional forms of transportation (e.g., foot, car, bicycle, horse, air, or boat patrol), and innovative forms of communication (including Facebook, Twitter, blogs, department websites, and other social media portals). Whether traditional or innovative means are used, the intent is to build relationships with members of the community.

Police are also responsible for responding to routine incidents while on patrol (e.g., car accidents or domestic violence situations) and to emergency situations (e.g., crimes in progress, natural disasters). Criminal investigations, the most sensationalized of all police duties, entail the collection, preparation, and identification of evidence, along with possible courtroom testimony. Crime scene analysis, a subset of investigations, is extremely important, but it accounts for only a small portion of police work. Lastly, police departments provide support services (e.g., interrogations, dispatch, training, evidence security, and internal investigations) within their own organizations and are responsible for problem solving crime-related issues within their jurisdictional boundaries.

The role of the police officer is potentially the most difficult among the three branches of the justice system, not only because of the danger associated with it but also because of constant public scrutiny. Furthermore, police officers are essentially on duty 24 hours a day, 7 days a week despite their officially scheduled shifts. They are expected to follow the law at all times, as well as inspire others to respect and obey the law. The stress associated with police work can be high and can have a detrimental effect on not only the officer but also his or her family, friends, and associates. The physical and psychological health of the individual, as well as relationships with others, can certainly suffer.

Employment Opportunities in Law Enforcement

Employment opportunities in law enforcement are plentiful and available on several levels, including federal, state, local, and private. Not only are federal law enforcement agents authorized to execute police functions (e.g., criminal investigations, search warrants, and arrests), but they also participate in inspection and regulatory activities. The Federal Bureau of

Investigation (FBI) is one of the most famous agencies in the world, and its agents work to protect the United States against terrorist threats and hostile foreign governments while also enforcing federal laws. Other well-known, crime-fighting federal agencies include the Drug Enforcement Administration (DEA) and the Bureau of Alcohol, Tobacco, Firearms and Explosives (ATF). Multiple other entities (Table 1.1) either are categorized as federal law enforcement agencies or have an enforcement arm. Each has an important role in the protection of the United States domestically and internationally. For instance, the Postal Inspection Service leads thousands of investigations a year involving mail and insurance fraud, while the Food and Drug Administration Criminal Investigations Office protects U.S. consumers from unsafe food, drink, and prescription medication.

Alternatively, a career in homeland security provides broad opportunities for new criminal justice graduates. There are positions in law enforcement, which can entail protection of the president and vice president of the United States, the nation's borders, and its transportation infrastructure. Mission support positions involve training, intelligence, civil rights, and fraud detection. In addition, homeland security careers involve protecting the environment as well as the economic interests of the nation.

Protecting America

Every state has its own law enforcement agencies, including but not limited to the following:

1. Local agencies, such as city and town police departments, county sheriff departments, university police departments, and school police

2. Highway patrols or state police

3. State bureau of investigations

4. Fish and wildlife agencies

5. Alcohol law enforcement agencies

Table 1-1   Federal Law Enforcement Agencies

Executive Branch*		
Department of Agriculture U.S. Forest Service	**Department of Health and Human Services** U.S. Food and Drug Administration National Institutes of Health	**Department of Labor**
Department of Commerce Bureau of Industry and Security Department of Commerce Office of Security National Marine Fisheries Service	**Department of Homeland Security** U.S. Coast Guard U.S. Customs and Border Protection U.S. Immigration and Customs Enforcement U.S. Secret Service	**Department of State** Bureau of Diplomatic Security
Department of Defense Air Force Criminal Investigative Services Army Criminal Investigative Services National Security Agency Police Navy Criminal Investigative Services	**Department of Housing and Urban Development** Protective Service Division	**Department of Transportation** Federal Aviation Administration Office of Odometer Fraud Investigation
Department of Education	**Department of Interior** Bureau of Indian Affairs National Park Service U.S. Fish and Wildlife Service	**Department of Treasury** Internal Revenue Service Investigations U.S. Mint Police
Department of Energy Office of Secure Transportation	**Department of Justice** Bureau of Alcohol, Tobacco, Firearms and Explosives U.S. Drug Enforcement Administration Federal Bureau of Investigations Federal Bureau of Prisons U.S. Marshals Services	**Department of Veterans Affairs** Veterans Affairs Police

*This is not an inclusive list of all entities under each department. Each of these departments also has an Office of the Inspector General.

Legislative Branch		
Library of Congress	U.S. Capitol Police	U.S. Government Printing Office Police

Judicial Branch	
Marshal of the U.S. Supreme Court	Office of Probation and Pretrial Services

Other Agencies		
Central Intelligence Agency National Aeronautics and Space Administration	U.S. Environmental Protection Agency U.S. Postal Service	Amtrak Police

States that operate under a centralized model combine the tasks of criminal investigations with highway patrol, creating a state police agency. States such as Michigan, Pennsylvania, and West Virginia use a centralized law enforcement model. On the other hand, states with a decentralized model include separate agencies that are responsible for highway patrol and criminal investigations. Many southern states, such as North Carolina and South Carolina, use this model by having a state highway patrol and a state bureau of investigation.

Local law enforcement agencies are those who protect city and counties, such as municipal police departments (city or town based) and sheriff offices (county law enforcement). City or town police chiefs administer police departments and have responsibility for overseeing their officers, whereas sheriffs represent the county through the use of deputies. In addition, medical examiners, campus police, and housing authority agencies are included under the category of local law enforcement.

Lastly, private protective services can be considered *private* law enforcement agencies because they generally enforce laws protecting property (i.e., theft, arson, and vandalism) and work to prevent high-technology crime (i.e., the theft of trade secrets from private companies). These are privately funded agencies that are responsible for the protection of specific businesses or other private interests, to include buildings, organizations, retail establishments, various kinds of facilities, intellectual property, and personnel. For example, security firms are often hired to protect airports, banks, schools, and shopping malls. In addition, loss prevention specialists are employed by every major retail store. In sum, there are multiple opportunities for law enforcement–related employment in addition to traditional police agencies.

The job of victim advocate provides an alternative employment avenue in the criminal justice field. Victim advocates perform a variety of duties, mainly coordinating and directing services for victims of crimes. Crime victims often need financial help, psychological and emotional services, and even protective housing. Victim advocates are especially important in domestic violence cases, as well as violent offenses.

Did You Know . . .

Thousands of students majoring in criminal justice and criminology have dreams of being a crime scene investigator or an FBI agent. Relatively few, however, achieve these goals. Keep in mind when considering a law enforcement–related career that there are multiple options available to you (see Table 1.1), and you should stay open to all opportunities. No matter what your career goal, it is imperative that you make an effort to become aware of employment eligibility requirements. For instance, anyone applying for work as an FBI agent must

(1) be between 23 and 36 years old, (2) hold at least a bachelor's degree, (3) have 3 years of work experience (unless able to prove certification in certain areas or demonstrate special capabilities needed by the FBI), and (4) not have a felony record or have defaulted on student loans. The FBI is often not specifically looking to hire criminal justice majors but instead may focus on individuals who possess computer science, biology, or accounting skills. Awareness of what your ideal job expects from you can keep you from wasting your time submitting job applications that are unlikely to be seriously considered.

Courts

Once an offender is arrested and charges are filed against him, he will then encounter the second component of the criminal justice system: the courts. Stakeholders in the American criminal court system work to protect the due process freedoms of anyone processed through the system. Criminal courts determine the guilt or innocence of an offender during the trial process and impose sentences on those convicted of crimes. In addition, they provide a check-and-balance system that works as a kind of oversight to the power exercised by police agencies and the corrections system to make sure no constitutional rights have been violated and to minimize harm to innocent parties and victims of crimes.

The American court system is a dual system, meaning that the federal and state court systems are separated. The federal government and most states operate under a three-tier system. On the federal level, district courts, tax court, and other entities are known as courts of original jurisdiction (trial courts). Appeals are referred to the Court of Appeals for each district, and then to the Supreme Court of the United States. In the state court system, the first tier is comprised of courts of limited jurisdiction, which are generally misdemeanor courts, drug courts, traffic courts, and family courts. Courts of general jurisdiction, the second tier at the state level, are the trial courts and may also act as probate courts (i.e., those dealing with wills, guardianship, etc.). Some states have an intermediate court of appeals, and all states have a court of last resort (or the state supreme court).

Employment Opportunities in Criminal Courts

Members of the courtroom work group are professionals involved in the routine activities of official court proceedings. In most jurisdictions, the following members of the courtroom work group must have a law degree: judge, prosecutor, and defense attorney. The judge presides over the trial, as well as associated pre-trial hearings and sentencing after the trial is over. She also rules on objections raised by attorneys, decides evidence admissibility, and may also decide guilt or innocence during bench trials. Prosecutors are responsible for representing the state (often referred to as "the people") during a criminal trial. They also make decisions on what charges to file, assist in police investigations, and gather evidence. There are federal, state, and county-level prosecutors, as well as assistants to the chief prosecutor. Defense attorneys, on the other hand, represent the defendant during trial. Defendants may hire their own attorneys or be appointed counsel by the court system if they are unable to afford one.

All of the previously mentioned positions require a team of employees to assist in daily work. Judges employ administrative assistants and clerks to help with motions, briefs, and other paperwork. Prosecutors and defense attorneys rely on paralegals, administrative assistants, file clerks, and receptionists to manage the day-to-day operations of their offices.

Other individuals who work in the criminal court system are not required to have law school training. Bailiffs, for example, are armed court officers who are responsible for maintaining order in the courtroom. Similarly, trial court administrators maintain the court schedule, case flow, and implement personnel decisions. The clerk of the court, on the other hand, is responsible for subpoenas, preparing a jury pool, and maintaining all evidence associated with a trial. Lastly, court reporters are hired to transcribe all words uttered during the trial process to create an accurate and thorough record of the proceeding.

It is also important to remember that the United States has a large juvenile justice system, which strives to rehabilitate minors who have been adjudicated (convicted) of crimes. This system builds upon the same kinds of positions mentioned earlier to effectively process juveniles through the system, as well as to provide them protective, educational, and social services when they are needed.

Corrections

The last phase of the courts process is the sentencing of the convicted offender, after which the corrections system takes over. The immediate goal of corrections is to implement a court-ordered sentence for those convicted of crimes, with the long-term goal of deterring an offender from committing crime in the future. Ideally, the criminal justice system aims to rehabilitate an offender by providing him or her with the tools needed to lead a crime-free lifestyle once released from confinement or while on release in the community.

The corrections system is responsible for the supervision of millions of Americans in various forms. The most commonly used form of corrections is probation, a judicial decision that entails serving a sentence in the community with certain requirements and restrictions. Probation officers are officers of the court, whereas parole officers fall completely under the umbrella of corrections. Parole, which in many ways is very similar to probation, is administered by the corrections system after an individual who was incarcerated has been released. Other forms of community corrections, such as community service, home confinement, and halfway houses, are also popular methods of corrections that are less expensive than incarceration.

The United States incarcerates more individuals than any other Western democracy. Many American jails and prisons are currently over their intended capacity. Whereas the majority of today's prisoners will eventually be released, more offenders are receiving longer prison sentences or even life sentences. In addition, prisons house persons on death row.

Another Visit to Solitary

Employment Opportunities in Corrections

Because of the large number of offenders in need of supervision, the corrections system is a huge employer in the United States. Probation and parole officers supervise convicted offenders and are generally responsible for meeting regularly with the offenders they supervise. This includes attending court hearings, making home visits, and engaging in various other activities that ensure the offender is adhering to the conditions of probation or parole. If the offender fails to meet these conditions, probation or parole may be revoked. Juvenile rehabilitative counselors perform the same functions as probation or parole officers but with children rather than with adults.

Correctional officers are extremely important stakeholders in the criminal justice system. Federal and state prisons, as well as federal, state, and local jails, require correctional officers to supervise offenders during incarceration. This can be a dangerous and stressful job, as a correctional officer spends his entire shift with convicted offenders who are generally not pleased with their situation. Correctional officers often respond to physical and verbal altercations, supervise meals and visitations, and provide counseling to inmates. In addition, they are responsible for the safety of the facility as a whole, which requires constant searches of the prison or jail, as well as the inmates, for contraband and dangerous objects.

Conclusion

It is hoped that after reading this chapter, you are even more excited about your choice to major in criminal justice/criminology. To obtain one of these fulfilling positions, however, you must first complete your degree requirements. As you explore this text, you will find many instructions and helpful hints that are meant to help guarantee your success during your time spent studying criminal justice, criminology, and security. You will learn about how to select classes, how to study and work with faculty, and how to best utilize the time available to you. You will also be shown how to apply for employment in the field, and you will be advised about some of the pitfalls that you should avoid. As the old saying goes, "Knowledge is Power," and it is our hope that this text will empower you through the knowledge it provides.

Discussion Questions

1. Were you aware there were so many opportunities for employment in the criminal justice system? Can you think of any not listed in this chapter?

2. What life decisions can you make now that will affect your eligibility for employment in your chosen field at graduation?

2 Maximizing Your Courses and Professors

Highlights of This Chapter

Working With an Advisor

Creating a Manageable Schedule

Developing Relationships With Professors

One of the greatest advantages of college life is choice. In high school, you had very little control over your class schedule, and almost everyone had to meet the same course requirements. Yes, you could choose an honors class or even decide to enroll in choir or band, but your class schedule was generally out of your control. Possibly the most unfortunate part of the high school scheduling process was the fact that you were stuck with whatever teacher taught a class, and that did not always mean compatible personalities, interests, or learning modalities between you and your instructor. However, once you are admitted and pay tuition at an institution of higher learning, the world is your oyster as scheduling choices can be vast!

This chapter discusses how to maximize your academic experience through class scheduling. Several excellent pointers for creating a class schedule that works for you are given, as well as tips for selecting the professors that fit your learning style. In addition, when faced with a professor who is not perfectly compatible with your personality, there are still many ways to have a positive experience from his or her class.

Step 1: Talking to Your Advisor

Upon entering school, you will be assigned an advisor. Before your first semester begins, universities and colleges will assign a college or school

Comparing Course Schedules

advisor who is well versed in the academic requirements of different majors. Somewhere around the time of your sophomore year, many institutions may reassign you to an advisor in your major department. However, no matter where your advisor is located, he or she is likely to be the key to your happiness. Often considered the guardian angels of undergraduates, advisors are the key to both organization and academic success.

A very important thing to keep in mind is the following: You are an adult. Therefore, you have many responsibilities to uphold. It is not the responsibility of your advisor to make all of your choices for you, but he or she will be an extremely important asset if you follow these simple rules.

Make an appointment with your advisor before registration begins. Classes can fill up very quickly, so waiting until the last minute to get an appointment will make it difficult for you to get the class schedule you need and the class times or professors that you desire. All universities and colleges, even if online, have advisors to help students prepare for the next semester. Keep in mind that once a class is full, the instructing faculty member is not required to allow you into that class. In fact, if you take courses in a physical classroom, it may be against fire code to allow one more desk in an already-full class. Many students have delayed graduation by at least one semester by simply forgetting to register on time—don't let this happen to you!

Arrive at the appointment on time. Advisors have set appointment times. Coming late or missing an appointment can deprive you of much-needed question and answer time with your advisor. Appointments can take place in a faculty member's office, online chat, or over the telephone. The time allotted (generally 15 to 30 minutes) goes by quickly, so make it a priority to use it wisely. Missing an appointment may result in you missing your designated registration time.

Be prepared for the appointment. This requires some extra effort on your part before the appointment. Look at the upcoming semester's schedule for class offerings and times, and review your study program's check sheet so you know what classes you still need to take. If you have a list of questions ready for your advisor about these kinds of topics, the appointment will go smoothly.

Follow up with faculty if your advisor cannot answer a particular question. For example, advisors do not necessarily know if Professor X gives four or five exams, grades on a curve, or requires a paper. You may need to e-mail individual faculty members about their requirements to determine if a particular class will work for you.

Step 2: Creating a Class Schedule

Generally, the first semester or two, your advisor may actually register you for classes.

However, it will generally be your responsibility to register for classes of your choosing after these initial meetings. Choosing classes can be an extremely stressful venture, so there are ways to help you create an ideal schedule. First and foremost, *work on getting your general education requirements out of the way.* Most schools require certain basic classes for all students, although there are usually alternatives within required categories. You may, for example, be required to take a basic class in social science, and your school may allow you to choose between a sociology class, a psychology class, a criminology class, or even an economics class. Similarly, math, science, and history may not be your favorite subjects, but everyone has to take them. Waiting until your last semester to take basic classes is not wise, as it not only can create issues with prerequisites for other classes but also can make a miserable last year filled with classes that may not be of special interest to you. Take a few general education courses each semester, as well as a class you will really enjoy related to your major (e.g., Introduction to Criminal Justice, Policing, Corrections). By the time you are finished with these core classes, you will be able to customize your schedule for fun upper-division and elective coursework.

When you get to the point in your academic career that you are able to concentrate more on your major classes, try to *select courses that will benefit your future career plans.* It is tempting to take courses that are regarded as easy or those in which the professor is known to be fun, but not all those classes benefit you in the long run. All major programs of study have required courses (e.g., Introduction to Criminal Justice, Courts, Theories), but criminal justice/criminology majors are also allowed to choose electives in their field of specialty. If you are interested in law enforcement, choose to take courses related to policing. Students interested in a career in corrections should take courses on community corrections, capital punishment, and related topics. Lastly, as much as this last suggestion may make you cringe, *take a writing class* if it is not already required. Writing class . . . on purpose? Are you serious? As you may already know, or you will know, all criminal justice careers require a large amount of writing. In fact, your writing skills can make or break an important criminal case against a serious offender. So, sharpening your writing skills is always a benefit and makes you very marketable.

Sample Class Schedule

In this class schedule example of the first two years of college, you can see the balance of general education requirements, interesting criminal justice classes, and less intensive physical education classes. Essentially, there is balance but not an overwhelming number of difficult or work-intensive classes each semester.

Semester 1 (14 hours)		Semester 2 (16 hours)		Semester 3 (13 hours)		Semester 4 (16 hours)	
First-Year Experience	1 hrs	Science	3 hrs	Gen Ed	3 hrs	Science	3 hrs
English	3 hrs	Science Lab	1 hrs	Gen Ed	3 hrs	Science Lab	1 hrs
Math	3 hrs	History	3 hrs	PE	1 hr	Gen Ed	3 hrs
Gen Ed	3 hrs	Gen Ed	3 hrs	Corrections	3 hrs	Gen Ed	3 hrs
Intro to Criminal Justice	3 hrs	Policing	3 hrs	Courts	3 hrs	Criminal Justice Core	3 hrs
PE	1 hr	Major Elective	3 hrs			Criminal Justice Core	3 hrs

On that same note, *be sure to maintain balance within your course schedule.* Do not take all extremely difficult and work-laden classes at the same time. For example, you may want to take your science class and lab (which many students find intimidating) along with a physical education course or an art class (which can be enjoyable and allow for your creativity to manifest itself). Overburdening yourself with difficult classes can affect your grade point average and cause burnout very quickly.

Your personal life requires consideration. *Maintain a balance with school and life that works for you.* If you know in advance you have to pick up your children from school at 3:00 p.m. every day, do not schedule classes during this period in the afternoon. Do not register for a high semester load and work 40 or more hours a week, especially if you have family life to balance. This sounds beyond obvious, but many students try to pack in as many class hours as possible so that they can finish in a shorter amount of time. Going to school an extra semester or two may help you maintain your own personal mental health as well as a healthy family life. In addition, if you work a job with shift schedule or unpredictable hours, you may benefit from enrolling in online classes through your local university or a completely online program. There are benefits of both, which we discuss later in the book.

Next, *create your perfect schedule . . . and then come up with a backup.* Design a schedule that contains your ideal days and times, classes, and professors. Remember, college allows you to begin classes at 8:00 a.m. or 4:00 p.m., so you have a lot of freedom to customize a schedule that works around your job or just personal preferences. However, even if many of your classes are offered online, you must be willing to budge a bit because some classes are only offered at certain times of the day or even once a year, so be prepared.

Some of this may sound obvious, but you would be amazed at how many students forego this simple suggestion: Take the classes you *need*, and give them priority in your schedule. Double-check to make sure you are registering for the classes you need to complete your major, and do not repeat courses that you have already passed. Keep in mind, however, that you will typically have a number of electives available to you to complete the total number of hours required for graduation. So, at least to a certain degree, you can be adventurous with your scheduling! If you are certain that you can meet your major requirements by the time you plan to graduate, then register for a class or two that truly interests you and that you normally would not have the opportunity to take, like astronomy, scuba diving, or painting.

If you are unsure of which professor is best suited to your tastes, ask around! Speak with your classmates or use that fantastic tool we are now so dependent on for daily life: the Internet. There are multiple rating websites and message boards that give student-provided descriptions of professors and their teaching styles. However, be wary of relying completely on these websites for your class choices. Generally, students who use these rating boards are either the biggest fans of a professor or had horrible experiences and want to vent. Most students who enjoy classes on a normal/moderate level do not use the rating websites (e.g. Rate My Professor or MyEdu). Instead, use social networking websites to your benefit. Post on your Facebook or Twitter a general question about a professor ("Any thoughts on Professor Smith?"). You will be amazed how many responses you will get in an hour or two. Lastly, you can always e-mail professors and ask to see a sample syllabus of a recent class or ask a particular question about style of instruction and class requirements. With this information, you can get a better understanding of how the professor plans to lead the class.

It is important to keep in mind that your ideal schedule may need to be modified as classes could get full during the registration period. In order to avoid complete and total panic, have a list of backup classes that you still need to take. If there is a waiting list for the class that was your top pick but that is currently full, put your name on the list. You will still have an opportunity to change your schedule before the semester begins and even into the first week or so (depending on your school's policy).

Helpful Advice From a Favorite Professor

Step 3: Developing Relationships With Professors_____

Your schedule is set, your books are purchased or e-books downloaded, and your pencils (or devices) are ready to write down every bit of important information in a class. The ideal experience is that you will love the professor, learn more than you can imagine, and get a great grade. Does that always happen? Well, no, of course not. At least, not every time. Unfortunately, all of us encounter faculty members we do not like or with whom we have communication issues. There are certain things we can do as students to improve our experience in the classroom and our relationship with our professors.

Keep in mind that most professors love to teach, enjoy helping their students, and truly want the best for you. Many think of students as their own children, so they love to see you succeed! The main reason for professor-student issues and communication problems is not because the professor does not like the student but because the student has not performed his or her responsibilities. Professors appreciate students who do the required class work, and they like being treated with respect and kindness, just as you do.

Keeping Yourself in Check

How you ever known a student who expected the professor to bend over backward to make sure the student's needs were met but refused to take any accountability of his or her own behavior? Everyone needs help now and then, but you have to uphold your end of any relationship if you want it to be successful. Listed here are a few things to avoid asking or saying if you want to maintain your professor's respect and confidence in you as a capable student.

1. *Is it in the syllabus?* If you can read, you can find out yourself. When are your office hours? Do you take attendance? Do you count all the exams toward the final grade? These are questions most likely in the syllabus, so double-check that handy piece of paper before asking any questions.

2. *My printer ran out of ink. My computer died. I had to work overtime.* Essentially, any excuse that tries to get you out of an assignment or exam (most likely because you waited until the last minute anyway) will not be viewed favorably by professors. Keep in mind they were students at one time and may even have used those excuses themselves, so they are on to you.

3. *I e-mailed you and you didn't answer.* Yes, there are absolutely those faculty who are not good communicators, but they are few and far between. If you e-mail a faculty member, it is reasonable to expect an answer from him within 24 to 48 hours. Remember, faculty are people too and have other responsibilities, so they are not sitting and waiting for you to e-mail.

4. *I got an A in this class in high school, so why did I get a C?* Expectations for high school students and college students are very different, so your A-level work in high school may not be considered A-level now.

5. *Can I get extra credit so I can get a better grade in this class?* If a faculty member gave you the opportunity to earn extra credit, she would have allowed every other class member the same opportunity, which means a lot of extra time grading on her part. Yes, you may not have gotten the grade you desired in the class (whether it be because you did not work as hard as you should have or you struggled to understand the information), but it is unreasonable to request extra credit.

6. *I missed class; did I miss anything important?* This is probably the most infuriating statement any student has ever uttered. If class was in session, important things were going on. Professors are not going to refrain from teaching just because you are not there.

First, *attend class.* This task is probably the simplest, most relevant, and easiest thing to accomplish. Yes, if it's a classroom-based class, there will be days when it will be hard to drag yourself to another possibly boring lecture, but the only way to master the material and to know what happens in class is to go! If it is online-based, it may be even more difficult to motivate yourself to go (the professor can't see you to know you aren't there) or the Internet is out again! Students who consistently miss class often complain about not knowing what is going on, but they are not being accountable for their own behavior. If you are going to miss an important exam or have an emergency, contact the professor as much in advance as you can to notify her about the issue.

Second, *read the syllabus*. It is the key to everything in the class. Due dates, project descriptions, attendance policies, and all the other important information you need to know are in that document. Before contacting a professor to ask a question about the class, be sure to check the syllabus first.

Third, if the syllabus does not provide the answer, then *e-mail the professor*. In Chapter 5, we will discuss proper communication with faculty and other professionals. However, as a general rule of thumb, write your e-mail in a format that resembles the following:

Dear Dr./Professor _____:

My name is _____ and I am in your _____ class this semester. I have a question about _____. Could you please let me know _____? Thank you in advance for your time.

Sincerely,

_____

In addition, if you would like to make a face-to-face appointment with the professor, request to do so during the professor's office hours (also in the syllabus).

Assuming that you have done everything on your end and treated your professor with respect, you should have a successful working relationship during the semester. However, there is the occasional faculty member who is not good at replying to e-mails, is dismissive of student issues, makes inappropriate comments, or is just plain cranky. How do you handle such situations? If you have legitimate problems with faculty, this is a serious issue because you, as a student, also deserve respect. If you have made continued attempts to contact and communicate with a professor to no avail, then the next step is to *contact the department chair*. Provide a detailed account of what has happened and not happened and of the issue at hand. If you are unhappy with the response of the chair, then *contact the dean of the college* and continue the conversation.

Case Study 2.1

Texas A&M University's associate professor Dr. Irwin Horwitz e-mailed his strategic management class, informing them that they were a disgrace to the university and would all fail his class. Dr. Horwitz reported being harassed in class, insulted, and cursed at by multiple students. In addition, he claimed to have witnessed cheating by multiple students. He voluntarily left the class and another instructor took over for the rest of the semester. Texas A&M University administration reported that the entire class would not fail collectively, but grades would be assigned individually based on merit and completion of requirements.

Should Dr. Horwitz have sent the e-mail, or should he have taken other measures to address the class? If you were a student in the class and received Dr. Horwitz's e-mail, what would you have done?

Moving Forward

Now that we have established the groundwork for beginning a successful semester, the next chapter provides instruction on the often-daunting task of note taking. Taking good notes during a class lecture can be an important key to ultimate success, as it determines the ability to absorb the information through studying later. If you cannot understand your notes, how are you supposed to properly prepare for the class and future exams? The next chapter will give you the key to successful class preparation through note taking and studying.

Discussion Questions

1. Discuss your experiences with your academic advisor. Have they been positive or negative?

2. Thus far as a student, what have you done to ensure your academic success? Have you failed to meet any of your responsibilities as a student?

3. Identify an issue you may have had with a faculty member. What did you do to resolve the issue? Was the outcome positive or negative, and why?

3

Effective Note Taking and Time Management

Highlights of This Chapter

Creating Useful and Understandable Notes From Class

Studying the Correct Information

Managing Your Time for Maximum Benefit

Picture this: You are sitting in class, scribbling furiously every word your professor says, and when class is over, you have NO idea what she just discussed for the past hour and you cannot understand your notes. Students often end up trying to capture every word that is spoken onto paper or into their digital devices instead of listening to what's important. Although your professors are full of knowledge, not every single word that leaves their mouths is important, and much of it is probably irrelevant to the grades you get in class.

The purpose of this chapter is to help you master the art of taking useful notes and then effectively retaining that information in usable form. We discuss how to recognize cues from the professor that indicate important information, as well as what information is not so important. This chapter will also discuss note-taking and studying strategies for maximum information retention.

Picking Up Clues From the Professor

How do you know what lecture information is important and which pieces are crucial to remember for the exam? Professors will often give the following clues when they are lecturing to indicate that students will again see this information in testable form:

Making the Grade

1. *Reviews from the previous lecture*—If your professor gives a review of the last class at the beginning of the new lecture, you will likely see that material again on an examination or in some form of assessment.

2. *It's on the board!*—Professors use chalkboards, whiteboards, or PowerPoint slides to highlight what they think is important in their lectures. If your instructor wants you to visually see it, you can bet that it's important.

3. *Emphasis*—If a professor puts emphasis on a concept through voice inflection, spending extra time on it, and/or giving examples about it, it is definitely noteworthy.

4. *Repetition*—Much like a parent, if a professor repeats something in class and seems to be looking straight at you, it is a clue that you should write it down.

5. *Lists and Diagrams*—A great way to relay information is through lists and pictures. Even if the artwork is bad, keep in mind your professor is providing you with helpful ways to remember important material.

6. *Summarization*—If there is time at the end of the lecture, a professor may review a few major points from the lecture. These are likely to be important takeaway thoughts that you should make note of and remember.

Keep in mind, every professor is different and may have his or her own special way of delivering information. Some professors will give you a study guide in preparation for exams, while others provide access to their notes or PowerPoint presentations. So, utilize the hints listed in the previous paragraph, but definitely consider the specifics of each class and the personal attributes of your instructors when making decisions about the best way to take notes.

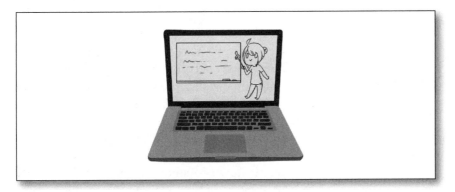

Electronic Learning

Making the Most of an Online Classroom

Obviously, if you are not in a physical classroom, it may make it difficult to pick up nonverbal clues from a professor regarding important information. Some online classes will have a group seminar in which students can listen to the professor lecture and have the electronic ability to "raise their hands" to ask questions, make comments, and participate in discussion. If you are in an online class without a seminar, we strongly recommend taking advantage of the discussion board or using e-mail to communicate with the professor in order to clarify any questions you have. Online classes without seminars will generally offer PowerPoints, outlines, or other written materials to assist you with comprehending the material. Use those to your benefit.

Stay on Task!

Time Management

Time management is using the practices, skills, and tools at your disposal to get more out of your time and improve the quality of your life. In other words, time management is appropriately using the precious free time you actually have to get everything done before your head hits the pillow and you start all over again the next day with a huge to-do list. Before we delve into time management dos and don'ts, take a few minutes to take the Personal Time Survey (Worksheet 3.1, page 33).

So, how did you do? Were you shocked by the number of hours you allow for study time, assuming you use all those hours studying? You and you alone know how much time you need to study in order to do well in your classes, so you may want to reevaluate the way you allocate your time to better maximize those short 24 hours we have each day.

All of us have challenges that make personal time management difficult. For instance, when we sit down to study, we may become easily distracted or bored by the subject matter. A common problem is for students to feel overwhelmed by the amount of material he or she has to cover and then not to have any idea about where to begin studying. In addition, some students may have some personal issues with family or friends, or have learning disabilities. No matter the issue, there are remedies and resources to improving your ability to manage time.

Suggestion 1: Set Goals

Once you have declared your major and begun working on your classes, you will have multiple semesters of courses ahead of you. Some of the classes you will take are extremely appealing, while others make a sunburn look like fun. Either way, you can get overwhelmed very quickly considering all the avenues and choices available to you. By setting goals, you can make your academic career more manageable and less nerve-wracking.

Setting the goal "Get My Degree" is very broad and not entirely clear, nor does it seem easily attainable. Instead, start with a few short-term goals that are not overwhelming. The time span is up to you, so this could involve a goal to be completed during the semester or within the next week. Next, list the steps necessary to meet those goals, as well as the subgoals beneath those if necessary. For instance, consider Figure 3.1.

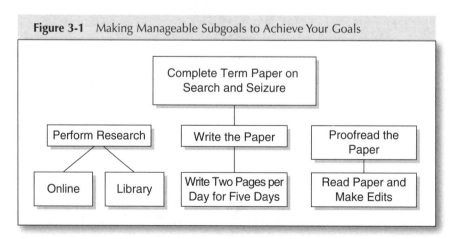

Figure 3-1   Making Manageable Subgoals to Achieve Your Goals

You can see how the daunting task of writing a complex term paper can be broken down into smaller, manageable tasks. This system of goal creation can be applied to a day-long task as well as to a year-long achievement. Goal creation is a good plan for undertakings that require multiple steps, such as applying for an internship.

_____ Suggestion 2: Put It on the Calendar

Have you ever gone to the grocery store to get a few items and forgotten something? You didn't make a list because you only had a few things to get . . . but you still forgot the orange juice! Let's face it, all of us have so many thoughts going through our minds, it's no surprise that some things slip our minds. There are multiple ways we can get our thoughts and tasks organized.

Some people find it useful to keep track of their "to-dos" on a calendar or in a planner. If you tend to have a lot of meetings, appointments, and due dates, it would be useful to get a planner that has each day with multiple time slots. For instance, many individuals prefer to write down their appointments on a tangible calendar so they can visually see what lies ahead for their day:

Tuesday

9 a.m.—Appointment with Dr. Stone

11 a.m.—Lunch with Jennifer

12:30 p.m.—Statistics exam

5:00 p.m.—Work

10:00 p.m.—Write two pages of term paper for literature class

---

Thanks to our ever-evolving technology, our smartphones, Internet providers, and search engines have excellent calendar abilities. For example, Google Calendar allows you to sync your smartphones with your online calendar, so you can make changes and additions that appear on both your computer and phone. It will even allow you to color-block time periods based on the type of entry and give you sound indicators to remind you of an upcoming appointment. If you prefer a cross-platform application for managing your calendar, one of our favorites is Sunrise Calendar—available on both Google Play and Apple's App Store and as a free Windows download.

Whether you choose tangible calendars, software-based, or online versions, it may help to see what lies ahead on your schedule. Most e-calendars allow you the option to view one day, one week, or even an entire month on your screen. Figure 3.2 shows a possible month view, allowing you to see what's ahead of you for quite some time.

Figure 3-2 Month-Long Calendar View

MARCH						
Sunday	*Monday*	*Tuesday*	*Wednesday*	*Thursday*	*Friday*	*Saturday*
	1	2	3	4	5 Angie's Party 11 p.m.	6
7	8 History Study Guide Due	9	10	11 Econ Midterm	12	13
14	15 SPRING	16 BREAK	17 NO	18 CLASSES	19 ———	20
21	22 Corrections Project Due	23 Work Training 9 a.m.	24	25 Mom's Birthday	26	27
28	29	30	31			

Sometimes we do not realize how much we have to do in a week or a month until we see the big picture. However, remember the point of creating a calendar is not to overwhelm you or feel as if you have absolutely no flexibility in your daily life. In fact, by prioritizing what you need to accomplish, you can provide yourself with more free time.

Another alternative is to make a "To-Do List" for each week. Many e-calendars allow for easy To-Do List creation and also include built-in reminders that can be set to varying lengths of time. Because a To-Do List provides the ability to check off (and dismiss) a task, we all get a feeling of accomplishment when using one. There is no one format for To-Do, but an example can be seen in Figure 3.3.

Figure 3-3 To-Do List

1. Take Spike for grooming.

2. Study for Chemistry 1 exam.

3. Write three-page paper for Policing Issues.

4. Buy Sarah a birthday gift.

Another method of organization is the development of a weekly goals list (Figure 3.4). In this type of organization, you allot certain periods of time for completion of the task, so you know in advance how much to plan when determining your schedule.

Figure 3-4 Weekly Goals List

Task	Time Allotment	Completed
Study for Criminal Theory Final	1 hour per day for 3 days	√ √
Grocery Shop	1 hour	
Clean apartment	2 hours	√
Complete Assignment 2 for Research Methods	3 hours	

After you've created a list of goals for the week, you'll then have the ability to work on those tasks at times of your choosing, and you won't feel as if you are constrained by a constantly scheduled life. In addition, you can (and should) reward yourself for getting something completed! Once you've achieved one of your listed goals, watch your favorite television show, grab a coffee, or go on a hike. Your week should have some down time, as everyone needs to recharge their batteries.

Procrastination Is the Enemy

Suggestion 3: Prioritize

It is midnight and you are just now able to sit down and start writing your term paper for your policing class, which is due tomorrow at 8:00 a.m. Is this paper likely to be the best thing you have ever written? Absolutely not, and if you are telling yourself otherwise, you are trying to fool yourself as much as you are your professor. The previous section discussed many ways to stay organized; however, even if you use the techniques discussed, you shouldn't wait until the last minute to work on important assignments. When creating your weekly or monthly objectives, consider the following questions:

1. *How much time and brain power is required to complete this task?* Going to the grocery store or cleaning your apartment may require the same amount of time as working on your lab report but not nearly the effort and concentration. Take this into consideration when scheduling those events, as you may want to give yourself some extra time to take a mental break.

2. *How much prep work is required for this task?* When you are writing a paper for class, generally it involves more than just sitting in front of the computer and banging out some words (or it should anyway). Most academic papers require research and critical thinking. When planning ahead, take into account the needed extra time and work.

3. *Do I need to proofread my work for classes before turning it in?* YES! YES! YES! No matter what you are doing, you should proofread it. A one-paragraph critique should take you approximately 5 to 15 minutes to proofread and make edits. Conversely, a 20-page report will take much longer and should be proofread several times before submission. It is smart to build time for proofreading into your time planning.

Suggestion 4: Focus

Have you ever done everything possible to avoid a task, especially for a class you loathe? Of course—we all have! However, avoiding assignments and study sessions will not earn you passing grades in classes. Sometimes we have to crack down and get the job done. To be successful, we need to focus. Take away the distractions! Take the distractions quiz (Worksheet 3.2, page 34) and consider your focus vices.

What was *your* number of distractions? Now that you know what distracts you, let's consider what you can do about keeping your focus. Obviously, if your children get sick or need dinner, you cannot ignore them. And yes, sometimes you do need to take a break to talk to your grandmother on the telephone—grandmas come first! But, if the majority of your distractions do not have to be performed immediately or are technology-related (i.e., texting, watching television), then these are likely just happy distractions to keep you away from what is more important. This is when you need self-discipline. Put the phone down—put it in the next room if necessary, or silence it. Alternatively, give yourself a 5-minute brain-break every 30 minutes to do something mindless and enjoyable. Keeping your focus for short time spans, with breaks intertwined, can help you maximize your time, produce excellent results, and avoid burnout.

Creating Effective Notes

Now that we have covered how to listen for the important information in a lecture, the next step is creating notes that will be useful and understandable. There are multiple ways that students are now creating notes, whether in hard copy or electronic version. This section covers some methods of capturing information.

Getting It Down on Paper

Many of us come from the "old school" where our notes were created with pen and paper and we did not have access to electronic means. Non-traditional students and those in online environments sometimes still prefer the pen and paper method so they can have a tangible product to review. In addition, some people prefer writing down notes because the process of writing helps them retain information better. As you are listening to the class lecture and utilizing the clues discussed earlier in this chapter, keep in mind a few rules that will be helpful in taking effective notes:

1. *Do not write down every word you hear.* This is neither time-effective nor necessary in order to do well in the class.

2. In addition, write *short sentences and use brief words.* This will make studying easier when you go back and review the notes.

3. If it helps, *create your notes in an outline format* complete with indentions to indicate subheadings.

4. If you are taking notes on paper, then *leave space between each line* so you can always go back and write details if necessary.

5. Lastly, whether you use paper or an electronic device, a *second color pen or virtual highlighter* is useful for marking particularly important concepts or lists.

Taking Notes With Technology

As an alternative note-taking method, many undergraduate students have been trained to use technology to assist with recording notes. In fact, many techno-savvy students find it difficult to find and record information any other way! There are so many different technologies that have been developed to assist students with recording information. They can be especially helpful for students who do not write quickly, have trouble hearing, or have professors who speak very fast.

Computer technology. Today's education system encourages the use of technology in the classroom, allowing students as young as those in kindergarten to become proficient with a computer. By the time they have reached college, students are able to use computers easily and have developed good typing skills in the interim. In fact, many universities are now issuing laptops or tablets to first-year students upon enrollment for classroom use.

Obviously, typing notes during a lecture is one note-taking method. Some students, however, prefer audio recording software to capture information during a class session. For instance, programs like OneNote and Evernote have audio recording and transcribing software for most operating systems, including Mac and Windows. Both allow information access on a smartphone or tablet. AudioNote and Notability record audio notes but can also convert what is recorded to typed notes. In addition, EndNote, a reference and bibliography builder, has an audio application that can also be uploaded to the normal program.

Sharing notes. Gone are the days of saving documents to a flash drive in order to work on projects and papers on different devices. Programs are now available that allow access to files from different locations, as well as provide the ability to share them with others. For instance, Google Docs are saved to a virtual drive on the Web, so you can access those files anywhere you can access the Internet. In addition, services like Dropbox allow you and other users to view and make edits to documents without having to e-mail them back and forth. Dropbox is a perfect example of a service that allows students to share notes from class.

Pen + Technology = A Happy Medium

What if you are a student who masters new innovations but still enjoys writing down your notes? Of course, those technology geniuses have created something for you! An electronic pen, or a stylus, allows users to write and draw on a tablet or touch-enabled computer screen. For instance, both Microsoft Surface Pro 4 and the Jot Script Evernote Edition allow placing electronic ink to tablet.

A Picture Is Worth a Thousand Words

The majority of cell phones, especially smartphones, are equipped with cameras that allow for excellent image capture. Grandma's birthday and your best friend's graduation party can be easily recorded and stored on your phone! After getting permission from the professor, many students will take pictures of PowerPoint slides or writing on a chalkboard or whiteboard to prevent missing important information. After class, the student can review or print off pictures and use them to create new notes or simply study from them. Some professors upload their PowerPoint presentations to an electronic board so students can print them off to follow along in class or use them while preparing for an exam.

Absorbing the Information

Since you have taken the time to create your notes, surely you will remember them for exams, right? Unfortunately, not all of us have the ability to remember everything we've captured on paper or elsewhere, and we require some intense studying time in order to be prepared. This section provides some helpful suggestions for remembering the information you wrote down in class.

1. *Review your notes on a regular basis.* If the information is particularly difficult to understand or if you are having problems remembering certain concepts, it is to your benefit to review the information periodically—even daily, if possible. Furthermore, if you know the information covered in the next class will build on the information provided during the previous class, be sure to review those class notes so your confusion does not build.

2. *Organize your notes.* Shoving random pieces of paper of various sizes in a notebook is a recipe for disaster. Keep your notes in chronological order in a notebook, three-ring binder, or organizational software for easy access and organization. Dating your notes each day is also a helpful idea.

3. *Participate!* Sitting in a chair and taking notes is only part of student success. Asking questions, participating in discussions, and being an active member of the classroom environment are extremely important. If your instructor is speaking too quickly or if you need a concept repeated, raise your hand and let her know. If you are confused about a concept, ask for clarification. The same rules apply to online classes, although the methods of participation may vary.

4. *Read the text . . . no, seriously.* Professors do not assign textbooks for torture or to make you spend your hard-earned money for an expensive doorstop. The information in the text accompanies the lecture, gives clarifying examples, and provides practice exercises to help with understanding. In addition, some professors will not lecture on every bit of information in the text but expect you to know it, so reading keeps you in the know.

5. *Set a study schedule.* Designate regular times to review notes, read, and study the same way you set a work schedule or plan to eat dinner. This will help you learn information on an incremental basis, but you will not be overwhelmed by trying to absorb a whole unit's material at once. In addition, study in a quiet place away from other temptations (e.g., television, video games, and cell phones).

6. *Don't cram before an exam.* Everyone has a busy life, whether it includes schoolwork, a job, family, children, or all of these things. In addition, studying for an exam is generally not an enjoyable activity, so it is easy to procrastinate. However, cramming for an exam hours before the test is never a good idea. You will not retain the information as well as if you studied the day before the exam and got a good night's rest.

Reaching Out

The next chapter reviews a form of learning that is taking the world by storm: online classes. As you move to the next chapter, consider the pros and cons of this form of learning and whether it can work for your lifestyle. Possibly you are thinking "I communicate all the time!" But are you doing it correctly, professionally, and without offending someone? So, take notes as you move forward to Chapter 4!

Discussion Questions

1. What type of note taker are you? Can you improve the way you take notes?

2. Have you ever had a professor who made it difficult for you to understand his lecture? What did you do? Is there anything you would do differently the next time this happens?

3. Generally, we are our own worst enemy. What is one way you sabotage yourself in regard to time management? How can you fix it?

WORKSHEET 3.1

Personal Time Survey

1. Number of hours of sleep each night _____ × 7 = _____

2. Number of grooming hours per day_____ × 7 = _____

3. Number of hours spent on meals/snacks per day (including preparation time) _____ × 7 = _____

4. Total travel time weekdays _____ × 5 = _____

5. Total travel time weekends _____

6. Number of hours per week spent on regularly scheduled events (church, clubs, etc.) _____

7. Number of hours per week for chores, errands, etc. _____

8. Number of hours of work per week _____

9. Number of hours in class per week _____

10. Number of hours per week socializing (online/offline) (be honest!) _____

Add up the totals _____

Subtract the above number from 168 – _____ = _____

The remaining hours are the hours per week you have allowed yourself to study.

WORKSHEET 3.2

Distractions Quiz

Check each item that has kept you from focusing on schoolwork.

Texting   _____

Talking on the telephone   _____

Social networking websites   _____

Playing video games   _____

Listening to music   _____

Entertainment/news websites   _____

Surfing the Internet   _____

Watching television   _____

Outdoor activities/sports   _____

Housework   _____

Friends   _____

Spouse/significant other   _____

Children   _____

Other   _____

How many did you mark?   _____

4

Online Learning

It is a fact that all undergraduate and graduate students are fully funded by their parents, do not have to work, do not have any family or childcare responsibilities, and can take classes whenever they want. . . . Wait, wake up from that dream! It's the complete opposite of reality for the majority of students. Most students have many life responsibilities that they have to consider when planning their academic schedules. As a result, attending classes that are scheduled for a specific time every week may not be conducive to your work schedule or children's events, especially if you have a full-time class schedule of 12 credit hours or more. Enter the convenience of online learning.

Originally, when online classes and online degrees were introduced, they were met with a lot of hesitancy. Many in the academic world had little respect for what was then called "distance education" and questioned the rigor of online classes compared to classes taught in the physical classroom. However, times have changed and universities now recognize the value of, and demand for, online classes.

Before we discuss all the benefits of online learning, it is important to understand that it is not an easier way to get a degree. In fact, for many students, it can be more challenging. Since you will not be in the physical classroom environment where you can freely discuss concepts with other students and your professors, you will likely have to work harder in a variety of ways (and normally that means writing a lot more). Additionally, online study requires you to stay motivated and to not procrastinate—challenges that can be extremely difficult when there are other pressing items on your

Where Do I Click?

agenda. This chapter explores the ins and outs of taking online classes and pursuing an online degree.

Categories of Online Learning

There are three main categories of online courses, but these can be combined depending upon the class and/or the university offering the courses. *Independent study/correspondence courses* are not formal classes and do not involve an enrolled group of students who spend the entire semester together. Instead, they are courses arranged between a professor and student, which involve either access to materials online (the more popular option) or materials that are mailed to the student. If the materials are accessed online, they are generally available in a password-protected area. These courses are completed in a certain time period that is preapproved by the professor (it may be a few weeks, months, or even a year) and are very useful when a student is interested in performing research, needs one last course to graduate, or is having serious scheduling issues that prevent her from enrolling in a normal schedule class. Often, assignments can be submitted when the student chooses as long as all of the assignments are completed by the due date.

These kinds of online courses can be extremely convenient for a student as they can be completed at the student's own pace. However, that convenience can also be a hazard, as many students will procrastinate working on assignments until the last minute, which decreases the quality of the work. In addition, turning in assignments all at one time, or near the course completion date, does not permit professors an opportunity to give feedback on a consistent basis, which would allow for improvement.

The second category of online learning is *synchronous courses*. With these courses, the students and professor are online at the same time in some form of chat room. There are a variety of audio-visual technologies that can be used for these classes. For instance, the professor may lecture in audio and the students respond via text by typing in a box on their computer screens. Or, professors may provide video lectures while students use headsets equipped with microphones to discuss concepts in real time. Professors can present PowerPoints, show videos, and engage in live discussions.

Synchronous courses have prescheduled lectures that take place on a regularly scheduled basis, generally once or twice a week. Assignments, discussions, and other activities are due at specific times throughout the course. This format is often used by universities that specialize in offering degrees completely online, such as Kaplan University or University of Phoenix. These schools target the working professional who is unable to attend classes on a regular basis in a physical setting. However, the disadvantage of synchronous classes is the set times of class meetings, which can be extremely inconvenient for students with professional and family schedules. Consequently, it may be difficult to attend every class session, especially since some students may be in different time zones. Although students can go back and listen to archives of lectures, doing so will not allow them to participate in real-time discussions with classmates or ask questions of the professor.

The last form of online learning is *asynchronous courses. Asynchronous* is a term used to indicate communication that is not simultaneous or that is intermittent. In such courses, each week generally has a theme (or topic) of concentration and runs from Sunday to Saturday, or something similar. Assignments and discussions are due by the end of each week, and students can complete them according to their personal schedules during the week. For instance, in a policing course, the theme for the first week might be the history of policing, and all assignments, discussion, and other activities would revolve around that topic and might be due on Saturday by 11:59 p.m. The next week, beginning Sunday at 12:00 a.m., would involve a different topic (e.g., styles of policing, purpose of policing) and would be addressed similarly.

This form of online instruction is popular and frequently used by online programs. It is also very convenient for students and professors, as coursework can be performed at their convenience, rather than having to schedule work or vacation around seminars (or missing the seminar completely).

Web-Based Educational Platforms

Universities that offer most of their courses in the physical classroom, but also have some online classes and perhaps a few online degrees, typically use a Web-based educational platform to host their classes. These platforms are similar to one another in many ways, but each has its own benefits to both the professor and the student. For instance, Moodle is a popular platform that provides an easy-to-use, customized interface. The dashboard, or main screen, allows users to navigate personalized files, activities, and even a calendar. Students can receive automated notifications of due dates, and instructors can track students' use of posted files.

Blackboard Learn is another popular platform that includes data analysis capabilities. Instructors who use it can analyze grades and course

Keeping Organized

interaction to help improve student performance. Users can take Blackboard Learn wherever they go—as long as they have a Web-connected device. Access is available on smartphones, iPads, tablets, and other transportable devices. Of course, laptop and desktop computers are also fully supported. Lastly, educational platforms such as WebCT or Sakai can be used by large and small universities or by their own designed areas.

Getting Prepared for the Online Course

Chapter 3 discussed some pointers on developing better time management skills. Such skills are extremely important when working with online classes. The first step is to compare your schedule with that of the online class. Some online universities offer intense learning experiences that last 6 weeks. They offer scheduled seminars each week on the same day and time. If you are taking a class with this format, you need to determine if your lifestyle will allow you to dedicate the time and effort needed to successfully complete the class. You may be better suited to a class that does not have a regular meeting seminar or that lasts over a 16-week period and is not so work-intensive. Once enrolled in your online classes, immediately put all due dates into your calendar (Web-based calendars that give notifications are excellent tools).

The next step is to prepare an environment conducive to success at independent learning. Determine where you will be doing your coursework, seminars, and other requirements. This can be your home, office, or even a coffee shop, but it is necessary to work where you will not be distracted. Children, jobs, smartphones, and many other things can easily divert attention from coursework.

Now you are all set and ready to learn! However, you have one final important and obvious requirement: a computer and Internet access. Although it is advisable that you own a computer to participate in online classes, your finances may not allow it. However, keep in mind that when you are using a publically accessible computer, like at a library, you are dependent on other's people's schedules, and the machine you need may not be available when you want to use it. So, don't wait until the last minute to complete a paper, as you may find the library closed or all the computers taken. In addition, it is important to have reliable Internet access. Of course everyone loses power now and then and nothing can be done about that. However, relying on the Wi-Fi at a fast food restaurant is not always your best bet. If possible, pay for Internet access at your home or be sure to find a reliable place to go online.

Components of the Online Course

No matter the format of your online course, it is likely to contain some common features. First, all online classes should include a *syllabus* that outlines the expectations for the course. The class title, meeting times, and location should be included on the syllabus. A brief faculty member bio, including his or her contact information and qualifications, should also be included. Most importantly, the syllabus will outline the requirements for completion of the course. It is important to read and reread the syllabus throughout the semester. A common complaint of faculty is that students will ask questions or complain about grading and policies that are clearly outlined in the syllabus. Ignorance is not bliss in this particular case.

Most online classes have *exams and/or quizzes* to test students on what they've learned. Online classes will often utilize timed quizzes/exams with 15 to 20 questions that are randomly drawn from a test bank containing dozens of questions. With this method, it is more difficult for students to cheat. Alternatively, essay exams may be used that require in-text citations to support the answers given.

Almost all online classes use some type of *discussion board* to allow for critical examination of a topic among students. Some boards require initial posting in response to a question (or set of questions) and may require responding to other students in the class. Contributions to discussion boards must be completed within a specified amount of time (such as a week). Other discussion boards may be held in real time, and either the entire class will be given a specific time to attend or students may be allowed to choose from several assigned options to participate.

Discussion Practice

Assume you are taking an online course in corrections. The theme of the current unit is sentencing, and your professor has asked you to identify whether or not the death penalty is an effective deterrent. In addition, you must respond to at least three of your fellow students' posts and support your answers with empirical evidence (not just your opinion). Would this be difficult considering the requirements of your personal life? Why or why not?

Assignment/activities are another option that can be used in online courses. These are not necessarily derived from assignments or activities that can be delegated in physical classrooms and may include short essays, debates, or reactions to *assigned readings* (book chapters, articles, and websites). In addition, *audio-visual assignments* are often used in online classes. Videos on YouTube, National Public Radio (NPR) podcasts, and government websites are just a few of the types of items that may be assigned for students to view as part of their class requirements.

The *dropbox* is the location where students turn in assignments or projects. Professors will most likely return assignments in the dropbox with comments, and students can see only their own dropbox. A *doc(ument) sharing folder* is the location where documents, files, and photographs can be shared with the entire class.

Online Class Decorum

The online classroom offers a multitude of options for communicating with others through writing and discussion. However, dependent upon the option chosen, there are appropriate ways to address your classmates and professors. As you will not have the opportunity to use verbal and nonverbal cues that you might use in a physical classroom, you must be mindful of what you say and how you say it.

Don't get too personal. Generally, most online classes allow for students to introduce themselves by providing some personal and professional information. A good rule of thumb is not to provide any information to online classmates that you would not provide to a group of strangers. Remember you are posting everything on the Internet, so technically anyone with enough skill can access it despite security precautions. It is absolutely appropriate to give a general overview of yourself, family, and career goals. However, avoid posting information like specific addresses, names, and other identifying information. For example, which of the following posts do you think would be most appropriate?

1. Hello, my name is Susan Merton, and I am married with three kids. My husband doesn't do much, and my kids drive me crazy. I love the color red and hope to be in the FBI one day.

2. Hello, my name is Susan Merton. I live in the Northeast and enjoy skiing with my family. After graduation, I hope to pursue a career in law enforcement.

Be personable. Personal is not the same thing as personable. The other students will respond to your introduction and what you say about yourself. In your responses, you do not want to be rude and shut them down with brief, impersonal comments. You can engage in friendly, open conversation without having to reveal your life history.

Take the discussion board to the next level. We can promise you that you will not receive top marks on any discussion board simply by posting brief, one-sentence comments and responses. Professors expect you to make substantive comments that evidence knowledge, contain factual information, and offer critical analysis. In other words, think about what you are posting! Rather than responding to classmates with "I agree" or "You are wrong," indicate why you have certain opinions and provide information that helps support your opinion. For example, if a peer indicates that drug offenders should be incarcerated without treatment, because the prison experience should be a punishment and not a country club, you might say:

> I appreciate your view, John, and I agree that when a person breaks the law there needs to be an element of punishment. However, I believe that when a person is incarcerated for drug use, he also needs therapeutic and medical treatment to acquire the tools needed to fight the addiction once released. Addicts have psychological issues associated with their drug use, and incarceration alone does not help solve these issues.

R-E-S-P-E-C-T. It is important that you be respectful of your classmates. Even if they make comments that are inappropriate, provide wrong information, or simply disagree with you, it is easy to get your point across and still be polite. While it is fine to disagree, never be threatening or hostile in your comments. In addition, address students by the names they provided in their introduction and your professor with the appropriate title (e.g., Dr. Thomas, Professor White).

In addition, be very cognizant of how your writing can be interpreted. It is very easy for someone to take offense to a comment that you may have intended as a joke. Keyboarding does not allow for verbal and non-verbal cues that you might use in face-to-face conversation. Typing in all capital letters, for example, can be perceived as yelling, which may evoke anger or aggravation in the recipients of your messages. Consider, for instance, the following discussion board post:

John Smith:	I fully support the use of the death penalty as I feel some people are so evil they should be put to death for their crimes.
Teresa Johnson:	ARE YOU KIDDING ME, JOHN? I COMPLETELY DISAGREE.
John Smith:	Teresa, you need to get a grip. I am allowed my opinion.

In this example, Teresa used language that John felt was insulting, and John felt that she was "yelling" in capital letters.

P for professional. It is very easy to give a bad impression simply by misspelling a word. All e-mails and posts should be checked for spelling and grammar issues before hitting the "send" key. In addition, your behavior should be held to the same standard as it would be in the physical classroom. Refrain from swearing or yelling at classmates or professors. In addition, as discussed in a previous chapter, refrain from using texting language or shortcuts and abbreviations. When you send an e-mail or post to a discussion area, write in complete sentences and spell out your words.

Follow directions. Do you know what one of the top peeves of professors is? It's that some students do not follow simple directions. Professors feel that students who don't follow straightforward instructions are not giving their class the attention that it deserves. For instance, online instructors may ask you to turn in assignments in the following format: last name_first name_assignment number (e.g., Smith_John_Unit 2 Assignment). You would be shocked at how many students completely ignore this kind of simple request. When students don't follow instructions, instructors can choose not to accept assignments and may give the student a failing grade simply for not following instructions. Make sure you take a few extra moments to review your course home page and note important directions from your professor before commencing work.

Conclusion

So what do you think? Are you ready to jump into learning in the 21st century? Online classes and programs are extremely beneficial to criminal justice practitioners. These are men and women who already have jobs and do not have the time needed to attend classes in the middle of the day at a traditional university. The option to earn a degree online provides them with an opportunity that they would not have had only a decade or two ago. It also provides them with the opportunity to earn the credentials necessary for promotions, raises, and other on-the-job benefits.

Discussion Questions

1. Before you read this chapter, did you have a negative or positive feeling about online learning? Have your feelings changed now that you have read the chapter?

2. Do you believe that everyone is capable of succeeding in an online environment? Why or why not?

3. Are there any criminal justice classes you believe would be difficult to take (or teach) online? Why?

5 Communicating Effectively and Applying for Jobs

The age of technology has made possible many wonderful things. Today, we can go online to socialize, do research, find recipes, apply for jobs, shop for just about anything, and even find love using any of the many matchmaking services. We can send quick messages via text rather than having to make long (possibly expensive) telephone calls. Many use the Internet to work from home, to further their education, and to earn college degrees. So, is there a negative repercussion to the ever-increasing use of technology in our personal and professional lives?

Unfortunately, the answer is yes. For one thing, technology allows us to cut corners in our communications, and the result can often be

First Impressions Are Important

disastrous and sometimes offensive. The purpose of this chapter is to provide simple, understandable guidelines on communication that you can implement with the individuals who are important to your career: professors and potential employers.

Communicating With Your Professors

Let's start off with an exercise. Assume a student has sent the following e-mail to a professor. What problems do you find with this form of correspondence?

> Hi Mr. Thomas! I have relly enjoyed ur class this semester ☺. How are ur kids? They sure are cute lol! I have a question about our final project. Do i need to prepare a visual aid?
>
> Thx! Jan

There are many things wrong with this e-mail, but let's go over some rules and guidelines for successful communication before we revisit what changes need to be made.

Who Is Your Professor?

Most of us prefer to be addressed properly by those around us. For instance, if you are a woman, being called "Mr. Smith" would be offensive. In addition, dependent upon cultural expectations, some of us prefer to have children address us formally with a "Ms." or "Mr." in front of our first or last names. Similarly, when addressing a faculty member at your university or college, it is important to recognize she deserves respect for her accomplishments in her chosen career field.

The majority of faculty members at universities have a doctor of philosophy (Ph.D.) or doctor of education (Ed.D.) degree. Such educational accomplishments confer upon them the title of "Doctor," which can be abbreviated as "Dr." No, these kinds of doctors cannot operate on you or prescribe medicines, but, just like medical doctors, they worked extremely hard and went to school for many years to become experts in their field. So, for such people it is appropriate to begin an e-mail with the following salutation:

Dear Dr. Hester:

Conversely, some faculty members have earned a master's degree (e.g., an M.S.) in their fields but have not earned the title of "Dr." However, rather than using the title "Mr." or "Mrs.," addressing these faculty members in the following way is appropriate:

Dear Professor Huling:

or

Dear Instructor Mullen:

You may be thinking, how in the world do I know what title to use? There are a number of ways to find out. First, look on the professor's webpage or biography on the university's website. Second, if there are sample syllabi online for that professor, check them out. Or third, ask the professor or another faculty member in the department who would know the proper title. If you still can't find the answer, err on the side of caution and start e-mails with the *Dear Professor* salutation.

Who Are You?

When writing an e-mail to your professor, it is important to keep in mind that you are not his only student. Your professor may have dozens, or even hundreds, of students in the current semester. In addition, he may have multiple sections of the same class, so do not assume he will immediately know who you are and where to find your information. So, it is helpful to give him a heads-up on your identity when you begin your e-mail. Consider the following opening:

Hello, my name is Susan Turner from your Intro to Criminal Justice class at 9:30 a.m. on Tuesday/Thursday.

By providing this kind of introduction, he can find your information quickly in order to better address your question (especially if you are asking about grades).

Why Are You E-Mailing?

It is great to have a friendly relationship with your professor, but realistically your professor is likely to have many students, so e-mail correspondence should be brief and to the point. In other words, keep the chit chat out of the e-mail and save it for office hours or after class. First, place a short blurb on the subject line of the e-mail correspondence (e.g. *Final Exam* or *Project Requirements*) so your professor knows why you are e-mailing and your correspondence can be separated from less important ones. Second, after your salutation and introduction, state the purpose of your e-mail in full, concise sentences:

What Are You Saying?

I am writing to inquire about our final project. Do we need to prepare a visual aid in addition to the paper?

If at all possible, your professor should be able to read your entire e-mail in one screen length.

There are a few other things to consider when writing your e-mail. *Refrain from texting language, cute symbols, and abbreviations.* Texting styles are spilling over into other forms of communications, such as e-mail, but it is important to remember that e-mail is NOT texting. It falls more into the realm of professional communication, so be sure you spell out all words in your e-mail and avoid smiley faces and abbreviations for words and phrases (e.g., lol, ttyn, brb). This kind of "language" may be fine for your friends but not for your professors. In addition, *proofread your e-mail.* Make sure all words are spelled correctly and that your e-mail makes sense. Nothing is more embarrassing than simple mistakes that could have been avoided. Such mistakes show that you did not care enough about what you are saying (or about whom you are writing to) to check your e-mail before sending it.

Lastly, *do not get an attitude.* You may be upset about your grade, treatment by a professor or fellow student, or any number of issues. However, assuming an attitude or getting confrontational with a professor is never appropriate and will almost doom your communications from the start. If your professor gets an attitude with you, take the high road! If your professor gets out of hand in communicating with you, you can always bring in another party, like the chair of the department or dean of the college, and you will always look better if you have maintained a professional style.

Keep in mind that there are some subjects that are not appropriate to discuss using e-mail. If you want to discuss a personal issue that will require some time to resolve, e-mail your professor and request an appointment. In addition, if you want to speak with the professor about your grade or a serious issue regarding the class, a face-to-face meeting is more appropriate than conversing over e-mail.

Signing Off in Style

Now that you have crafted the perfect e-mail, it is important to end the e-mail on a positive and appropriate note. Once you have written the body of the e-mail, it is nice to show your appreciation for the professor's time. You can do this in a few different ways, depending upon the content. For instance, if you are asking to meet with the professor, provide several days and times that are convenient for you. A statement such as "I would like to meet with you on Thursday at 2:00 p.m." insinuates that you feel as if the professor has no obligations other than to meet with you. Conversely, giving several days and times allows you and your professor to decide on a time that works for both of you. Another scenario involves requesting a professor to review a draft of a paper. It is appropriate to end the e-mail with "Thank you in advance for your time."

Lastly, sign the e-mail with a polite ending, such as "Sincerely," followed by your name and identifying information. This identifying information should be university-related (not social security or credit card numbers), such as a student identification number or class information. By signing off in that manner, you are reminding your professor of your identity:

Sincerely,

Jonathan Young

Eagle ID: 4893848985

The Final Product

Remember the atrocious e-mail that began this chapter? Once we have applied all our dos and don'ts, this is what the revised product should look like:

> Dear Dr. Thomas:
>
> Hello, my name is Jan Smith from your Intro to Criminal Justice class at 9:30 a.m. on Tuesday/Thursday. I am writing to inquire about our final project. Do we need to prepare a visual aid in addition to the paper?
>
> Thank you in advance for your time.
>
> Sincerely,
> Jan Smith
> Banner ID: 67941679

Can you see how a professor would respond better to this type of communication?

As you continue through your academic career, there will come a time when you will have to communicate with professionals in the field. Many undergraduates in criminal justice/criminology are required to do internships, and eventually you will likely be seeking employment in a criminal justice–related agency. When communicating with other professionals, most of the rules of communicating with professors that we have just discussed still apply. The next section addresses appropriate communication with those individuals.

Point to Remember

It is important to remember that professors are people too! They have personal and professional lives and have experienced a lot of the things you are currently experiencing as a student. You may be surprised how sympathetic they can be to struggles you are having, but do not take advantage of that humanistic quality. Lying to a professor or making up an excuse can ruin your reputation if you are discovered. Honesty is always the best policy—professors will respect you for it much more than making up a lie.

Communicating With Professionals: E-Mail

Let's start off with an exercise. Assume your friend will be graduating next month with a degree in criminal justice and is currently applying for jobs. What problems do you find with her correspondence, shown below?

Angela:

My résumé is enclosed for the corrections officer position. I am excited to get an interview and talk about my skills.

Thanks,
John Hudson

There are many things that are wrong with this e-mail, but let's go over some general rules and guidelines to good communication before we revisit what changes need to be made.

Who Are You E-Mailing?

Composing e-mails to professionals can be tricky, especially when you do not know the person. The discussion in the previous section with regard to addressing someone properly also applies here. It is appropriate to address a professional with her designated title rather than first name. Even if you happen to know the person on a personal level, now is the time for a professional approach. For instance, if you are applying for a job in law enforcement and the applications are to be directed to Sergeant Michael Williams, your salutation should be: *Dear Sergeant Williams*. In other words, if there is a title associated with the person (e.g., Corporal, Dr., or Senator), use that designation. Otherwise, use of Mr. or Ms. is appropriate in the salutation heading.

Who Are You?

When writing an e-mail to a professional, it is important to keep in mind that you are likely not to be the only one who will communicate with this person today. Whether you are applying for a job or simply requesting information about a particular organization, you need to identify yourself. Consider the following opening:

Hello, my name is Marian Davis and I am an undergraduate student of Criminal Justice at Smith University.

or

Hello, my name is Thomas Anderson and I recently graduated with a Bachelor of Science in Criminology from Hudson College.

With this kind of an opening, you have introduced yourself in a friendly and professional way.

Why Are You E-Mailing?

As mentioned earlier, now is not the time for chit chat. Instead, you need to get right to the point and make yourself stand out. After your introduction, you should state the purpose of your e-mail, being as specific as possible. For example, if you are applying for a job, indicate the job title and where you heard about the position:

The purpose of this e-mail is to apply for the position of police officer at the Avon Police Department in Avon, NC, as advertised in the Outer Banks Gazette. *I have attached my official cover letter and résumé for your review and consideration.*

The cover letter (discussed later in this chapter) should contain a more thorough outline of your qualifications. If you are requesting information or an appointment, consider the following language:

The purpose of this e-mail is to request a telephone conference with you regarding the Justice Reinvestment Act. I am interested in doing my thesis on this piece of legislation and would like to discuss the impact it has had on our state's corrections system.

Lastly, the rules discussed earlier also apply to e-mails with professionals. *Refrain from texting language, cute symbols, and abbreviations,* and *proofread your e-mail.* Make sure all words are spelled correctly and your e-mail makes sense.

Signing Off in Style

Now that you have crafted the perfect e-mail, it is important to end the e-mail on a positive and appropriate note. Once you have written the body of the e-mail, it is nice to show your appreciation for the professional's time and consideration. You can end the e-mail with "Thank you in advance for your time, and I look forward to speaking with you soon." Lastly, sign the e-mail with a polite ending, such as "Sincerely," followed by your name and your credentials if applicable. And don't forget to proofread before hitting "send."

The Final Product

Remember the atrocious e-mail from earlier in this chapter? Once we have applied all our dos and don'ts, this is what the revised product should resemble:

Dear Sergeant Williams:

Hello, my name is Thomas Anderson and I recently graduated with a Bachelor of Science degree in criminology from Hudson College. The purpose of this e-mail is to apply for the position of corrections officer at North Kern State Prison as advertised in the California Department of Corrections & Rehabilitation newsletter *Rehabilitation Today*. I have attached my official cover letter and my résumé for your review and consideration.

Sincerely,

John Hudson

Depending upon the situation, the e-mail we just created may be sufficient for your needs. However, if you are applying for a job or an internship, you will be required to write a cover letter and prepare a résumé for potential employers to review and consider. The next section discusses appropriate techniques to create these documents.

Go Out and Get a Job!

Applying for Jobs and Internships

Creating a Cover Letter

The cover letter can propel you into instant consideration for a job or internship, or it can immediately send you into the trash pile. This quick change of course can occur not necessarily because you aren't qualified but because your letter isn't very well written or because you have so many typos in the first paragraph that an employer assumes you can't communicate well. Writing a cover letter can be an easy task, but it is important to include the necessary contents and follow the rules for appropriate content. A cover letter should introduce you to the employer and describe how you would be an excellent fit in the organization. It should show how you are qualified to assume the responsibilities of the position for which you are applying. In addition, it should demonstrate your knowledge of the organization, as well as your ability to communicate well and coherently.

Let's go over each section step by step, starting by viewing a sample cover letter. This cover letter (Figure 5.1) is written by a recent criminal justice graduate applying for a victim advocate's position.

The first section of a cover letter is the *heading*, which includes the sender's address, the date, and the address of recipient. Cover letters should be written single-spaced in a 12-point font that is not unusual. Appropriate fonts include Times New Roman, Arial, and Courier New.

Figure 5-1   Cover Letter Example

126 Firewood Lane
Dover, Delaware 19901

April 23, 2017

Kent County Courthouse
Attn: Mallory Johnson
414 Federal Street
Dover, DE 19901

Dear Ms. Johnson:

My name is Kathy Goring and it is with pleasure that I apply for the position of victim advocate coordinator for Kent County, as advertised in the *Dover Gazette*. Based on my academic training, as well as my experience in the field, I am highly qualified for the position and would be an asset to victims involved in the criminal justice system in Kent County.

In May 2016, I graduated from the University of Delaware with a Bachelor of Science degree majoring in criminal justice with a social work minor. During my studies at the University of Delaware, I took courses that would greatly assist me in performing responsibilities associated with the position, including Victimology, Court Services and Applications, and Management of Grief. These courses made me knowledgeable of the three facets of the criminal justice system, especially the responsibilities relating to crime victims and their families: finding resources, representation in court, and providing emotional support. My verbal and written communication skills are quite good, earning me high grades in all my writing and communication courses. In addition, my internship at the Kent County Courthouse in the district attorney's office allowed me to learn court operations in the county, as well as network with the court stakeholders, both of which give me insight into the responsibilities of the currently available position.

Thank you in advance for considering me for this position, and I look forward to speaking with you. I have enclosed my résumé for your review. Should you have any questions or would like to schedule an interview, please contact me at kgoring@hotmail.com or 123-456-7890.

Sincerely,

Kathy R. Goring
Enclosure

Your address should include only your address, not your name. A blank line goes between the address and the date you are sending the letter, and another blank line goes between the date and recipient's address. Your cover letter should always be sent to a specific person or department, and that information will likely be indicated in the job opening announcement. If it is not indicated, addressing the letter to Human Resources or Hiring Committee is a good option.

The second section of a cover letter is the *introduction*. Provide a blank line between the recipient's address and then begin with a salutation (Dear Ms. Johnson:). After another blank line is inserted, begin by discussing who you are and why you are writing. It is appropriate to note where you heard about the job, whether it be from a person, online advertisement, or career fair. Next, provide a brief discussion of the contents of your letter (a summary) and what the reader can expect to hear about more in detail in the upcoming paragraph.

The second paragraph of the letter is the *persuasion or argument section*. This is where you sell yourself as a candidate. Discuss your educational and vocational qualifications. Explain how your qualifications demonstrate that you are an ideal candidate for the position (noted in the advertisement) and the mission of the organization. It will impress the hiring committee if you demonstrate that you have done research about the organization and that you are knowledgeable about their goals and operations. In this section, you do not have to discuss every aspect of your résumé, but you should provide an overview of how your experiences and qualifications make you the perfect candidate for the job. If you have no employment experience in the field, it is a good idea to discuss internship and volunteer experience.

Finally, your *closing paragraph* should reiterate your appreciation for their considering your application, as well as provide your contact information in the event they want to interview you. It is important to provide contact information you actually use! For instance, give the e-mail address you regularly check and be sure the e-mail address is professional. An e-mail address such as steelersrule@hotmail.com or chucksgirlfriend@yahoo.com is NOT appropriate. Instead, use your academic e-mail address or create a basic e-mail address similar to the one in the example e-mail presented earlier in this chapter. Many e-mail services are free, so take advantage!

After you close, there are a few very important things to do. First, proofread! Read and reread the draft for spelling and grammatical errors. Ideally, walk away from the letter for a day or so before you proofread. That way, you will have a fresh set of eyes to find items that could be better written or to uncover mistakes. Second, your closing signature should be "Sincerely," followed by three blank lines and then your name. Once you print the letter, you will sign your name between the two. Then, if enclosing a résumé and/or other requested documentation, put the word "Enclosure" directly under your name.

Designing Your Résumé

You are now one step closer to securing that position! The next step is to create a résumé. There are multiple types of résumés, but, as a new graduate with little to no experience in the criminal justice field, it is most likely that you will be creating an entry-level résumé. Your résumé should be a brief summary of your experiences, academic history, and other important skills and qualities. Entry-level résumés should be relatively short—generally one or two pages. This way the employer can quickly determine if you are qualified for the job. Figure 5.2 is an example of an entry-level résumé.

Figure 5.2 provides a guide to anyone preparing to enter the job market. Each heading is clearly marked and organized in understandable fashion. Keep in mind the résumé is in a good, readable 12-point font. In addition, all the information is on one page. Each résumé you send out may need to be altered in various sections depending upon the job requirements. For example, if you apply for both a law enforcement position and a clerk of courts position, you may want to highlight different coursework.

At the top of the résumé is the applicant's name and contact information, which is also provided in the cover letter. The first section, Education, should include the institution you are currently attending or have graduated from. You should also include your graduation date (or expected graduation date if you have not yet finished). List your degree and any relatable minor and/or major coursework to the position for which you are applying. This may need to be customized for each application and should be limited to three or four classes. Lastly, only include your grade point average and status if it is notable. For example, a grade point average over 3.0 is worth noting and if you graduated cum laude (or higher) or with special honors, that should be noted as well.

The next section, Work Experience, can be tailored depending on your qualifications. If you have any work experience that is relatable or similar to the job, place it under *Related Experience*. If you do not, that is nothing to worry about! You can demonstrate you are still qualified and dependable by listing any work experience you have, as well as volunteer experience. Employers are looking for well-rounded candidates, not necessarily the person with the most years of experience. Under this section, include the name and location of your employment and your dates of employment. List your official title(s) and your responsibilities as an employee. Note that when you list the responsibilities, keep the first words of the lines in the same tense. In the example in Figure 5.2, the responsibilities in the internship section (under *Related Experience*) are described in the past tense because the applicant no longer works there. However, she is still an employee of Trudy's Jewelry (under *Other Experience*), so her verbs relating to that position are in present tense.

Volunteer experience is another section that can be added to an entry-level résumé, especially if an applicant does not have much employment experience. It is not unusual for full-time students to focus on studies and

Figure 5-2 Entry-Level Résumé

KATHY GORING

126 Firewood Lane, Dover, DE 19901
123-456-7890
kgoring@hotmail.com

EDUCATION

University of Delaware   Graduated May 2016

Bachelor of Science in Criminal Justice

Minor: Social Work

Cumulative GPA: 3.86

Related Coursework: Court Services and Applications, Management of Grief, Victimology

WORK EXPERIENCE

Related Experience

Kent County District Attorney's Office, Kent County, DE   Jan–May 2016

Intern

Responsibilities:

- Prepared evidence for court hearings and trial
- Assisted district attorney with correspondence to witnesses and defense attorneys
- Assisted in depositions

Other Experience

Trudy's Jewelry, Dover, DE   April 2014–present

Assistant Manager

Responsibilities:

- Train new employees
- Manage payroll
- Prepare orders for stock

VOLUNTEER EXPERIENCE

YMCA Kent County   March 2013–2014
Holly Hills Baptist Youth Group Leader   January 2015–present

COMPUTER SKILLS

Microsoft Office, SPSS, STATA

REFERENCES

Available upon request

not work during their undergraduate careers. However, many students volunteer for professional organizations, participate in community service, and are active members of extracurricular groups. It is important to list these activities and memberships because it indicates the ability to be a well-rounded and involved member of the community while simultaneously pursuing an academic career.

Another important section can be noted as Skills. If you are applying for a job that requires computer skills, it is important to note your proficiency with programs or Web design. Or, if the job requires proficiency in a foreign language or firearm experience, list that as well. Lastly, under the References section, note that your references are available upon request. This saves space for more valuable information.

Other examples of résumés include chronological résumés, which are used by seasoned applicants. For instance, if you have been a police officer for 10 years at two different locations, you would list that information before noting your recent education. However, most new graduates do not have that kind of experience and will need to place emphasis on other areas. Remember, you have to create a résumé that shows why you would be a great employee! Do not fill it with unrelated fluff.

Should I Include It?

If you are unsure about the usefulness of including certain information on your résumé, ask your professor. Volunteer experience or certain skills may be completely relevant for certain types of job applications but wasted space on others. In addition, you may not need or want to include your high school graduation information. If you graduated with high honors, it may be important to include. However, if you have graduated from college, an employer can assume you also have your high school diploma or GED, so it is unnecessary to include it on a résumé. There comes a point in your educational and professional career when high school experiences are irrelevant.

Discussion Questions

1. Explain a time that you felt you communicated with a professor or professional in an inappropriate way. What were the repercussions?

2. Think about your ideal career. What can you start doing now to help your chances of getting that job?

6

Writing Styles in Criminal Justice

Throughout your coursework and your criminal justice career, you are going to be asked to write many things. A common misconception of undergraduates in the justice field is that there is no need to learn to write well. This is completely wrong! Workplace success requires good writing skills. The purpose of this chapter is to discuss some of the forms of writing you may encounter during your academic career. We will also provide a few examples of good workplace writing.

Making the Grade!

Academic Writing

You have begun a new semester and anxiously flip through the syllabus to see if your professor is going to require a written paper. To your dismay, she is requiring a paper, and it has to be 10 pages long! Is she crazy? Who can write a 10-page paper? Before you launch into a panic attack, read the material in this chapter. Doing so will provide you with helpful information about how to write successfully.

Creating an Outline

Before writing the first paragraph, it is important to develop a concise outline for your paper. Much like an architect's blueprint for a building, an outline allows the writer to create a plan for the essay and ensures that all the necessary materials will be included. There are multiple forms of outlines, but one of the most popular is the alphanumeric outline.

Imagine that your professor asks you to write about a cybercrime that is interesting to you, so you choose cyberbullying. In an alphanumeric outline, you will designate main headings in the essay with a Roman numeral, and underneath each main heading, subheadings relating to that topic will be listed. An example of how this outline might look can be seen in Figure 6.1.

Choosing a Point of View

One of the important things to know about your paper is whether the professor wants it written in first or third person. If this bit of information is not provided in the assignment, ASK! The two writing styles are very different and using one rather than the other could make the difference between a good and a bad grade. Writing from the *first-person point of view* involves using first-person pronouns, such as *I* and *me*. As we go through primary education, we are essentially taught to write in this format. It involves an active voice. For example, "I think procedural justice is very effective," or "In my opinion, we should open a program to reduce recidivism in my town." When it comes to opinion-based essays, this type of writing comes naturally. However, it is not always acceptable for writing in higher education.

The *third-person point of view* is commonly employed in academic writing. It involves using third-person pronouns, like *he, she,* or *it*. As it is a more formal form of writing, you may use it to explain the contents of an empirical study. For example: "This study investigated the likelihood that drug use would increase deviant behavior in juveniles."

Finding Credible Sources

Let's face it—today's undergraduate students generally rely on the Internet to find information. If it's not online, it is too much of a hassle to

Figure 6-1   Example Outline

Cyberbullying

I. Definition of Cyberbullying

    A. Comparison of physical versus electronic bullying

    B. List and define different forms of cyberbullying

II. Victims and Offenders

    A. Characteristics of victims

        1. Typical victim features

        2. Psychological effects on victims

    B. Characteristics of offenders

        1. Typical offender features

        2. Male versus female cyberbullying behaviors

III. Policies and Legislation

    A. Contemporary court cases that influenced cyberbullying legislation

        1. Amanda Todd

        2. Megan Meier

        3. Tyler Clementi

    B. State and federal legislation

    C. School policies

find it. It may be advisable to use books or printed references. But if we refuse to use anything but the World Wide Web, let's take advantage of it!

Every university and college, whether online or physical, has a library at its students' disposal. We can easily find credible information on the library website by doing some simple searches. Below the search box, you will likely see an option of "peer-reviewed" to select during your search. Click on that! By choosing items that are peer-reviewed, you will pull from a plethora of credible, empirical research that passed the scrutiny of experts in the field before it was published. In addition, if you want to do a thorough job of research, check out a book! When doing so, look for texts that are written or edited by notable experts in the field.

If you find the need to search outside of your school library, there are multiple search engines available to you online. However, remember that sources acceptable for use in academic writing often include only websites where information is fact-based and does not consist of opinions.

Table 6-1   Sources of Criminal Justice Data

Information Source	URL
Administrative Office of the U.S. Courts	http://www.uscourts.gov/about-federal-courts/judicial-administration
Bureau of Justice Assistance	https://www.bja.gov
Bureau of Justice Statistics	http://www.bjs.gov
Bureau of Prisons	http://www.bop.gov
National Criminal Justice Reference Service	http://www.ncjrs.gov
Office of Juvenile Justice and Delinquency Prevention	http://www.ojjdp.gov
U.S. Department of Justice	http://www.justice.gov
U.S. Supreme Court	http://www.supremecourt.gov

Government reports, unbiased statistical analyses, and some news stories can be considered credible options. Popular criminal justice–based websites that students use are shown in Table 6.1. In addition, websites from free peer-reviewed journals and credible institutions like hospitals and universities can also be used.

Have you noticed that Wikipedia has not been listed as a credible website? That's because it is not! While Wikipedia and other Wiki sites can contain a lot of good information, anyone can access and edit it. This makes the information that's available there less than credible. In addition, private blogs, social networking website pages, and other similar websites are not acceptable places to find information.

Essay Styles

Argumentative Essays. Argumentative essays are writings that take a position on a particular topic or issue. Often assigned as a final paper or capstone project, argumentative essays involve searching for empirical evidence, statistics, and other studies that support your stance. It is not enough to state "I think this is stupid" and leave it at that. For example, your professor may ask you to choose a side regarding the death penalty. If you are against capital punishment as a sentencing option, then it might be appropriate for you to argue that it is not an effective deterrent of homicide. Multiple studies have shown that states that make use of the death penalty do not have lower homicide rates compared to states that do not have the death penalty. Arguing from a factual standpoint supported with evidence provides a sounder argument than just stating your morals and beliefs—and that's usually what your professors will be looking for.

The introductory paragraph of an argumentative essay should include a thesis statement regarding your stance on the issue. This statement should be as narrow as possible in order to provide an effective argument. For example, in an essay on capital punishment, the thesis statement could be: *Based on a multitude of empirical research, the death penalty has been shown not to be an effective deterrent of homicide.* The body of the essay should then consist of a discussion of studies, government reports, and other credible evidence that support your argument. It is completely appropriate to address the other side of an issue, such as support for the death penalty, and mention a few reasons why people hold this opposing opinion. Your concluding paragraph should emphasize the main points of your argument, and you should wrap up your paper with a firm statement in support of your position.

Descriptive Essays. Descriptive essays give students quite a bit of artistic freedom when it comes to writing. In assigning a descriptive essay, the professor is asking you to describe something. These types of essays should include clear language—words that make the reader picture the object, person, or place in his mind. Use words based on your five senses. For example, if you were to describe one of the older prisons built under the Auburn system that are still open, you might discuss the oppressive stone walls and the sharp razor wire encircling the facility. You might also say how the inside of the prison smells of cleaning fluid and sickness, causing visitors to feel uncomfortable and depressed.

Narrative Essays. Narrative or informative essays can be written in two different ways. First, the writer may want to tell a story, such as one about the first time he rode a bike. Using the pronoun *I* is acceptable in this type of writing. Narrative essays can also provide information about a topic and can discuss things such as mandatory minimum laws. This second view does not allow for opinions, only facts. It should be written in the third person. Either way, these essays should be clearly written and should contain a thesis statement.

Utilizing APA Style. As a student of higher education, you will encounter different types of writing styles and citation format. Each academic discipline has its own preference. For instance, English instructors generally request Modern Language Association (MLA) style for writing assignments, while sociology classes utilize the American Sociological Association (ASA) style. Criminology and criminal justice researchers have adopted the style developed by the American Psychological Association (APA). What follows is a discussion of the basics of APA style. However, for a complete discussion of appropriate citation styles and formatting for every type of reference, please consult the APA manual (*Publication Manual of the American Psychological Association*) or visit the APA website at www.apastyle.org.

Writing with APA style requires a specific paper format. For printed papers, margins should be 1 inch on each side and use 12-point Times New Roman font. Each page should have a running head, which entails a shorter version of the paper title flush left with the page number flush right. The title page (the first page) should also include the title of the paper, author name, and institutional affiliation centered in the middle of the page. The second page is an abstract page, which should consist of one double-spaced paragraph (no more than 250 words) that summarizes the contents of the paper. Essentially, the purpose of an abstract is to give the reader a quick snapshot or review of what the entire paper has to offer. If a research study is being described, then the abstract should include information on the purpose of the study, research design, analysis and results, and findings of the study. Abstracts are a quick way for readers to decide if a particular article is worth reading or if their time might be better served by reading another manuscript.

The body of the paper will begin on page 3, and length is obviously up to the writer and/or the professor. The majority of essay styles that we've already mentioned require an introduction, body, and conclusion for the paper. Empirical studies involving data collection and analysis require specific sections that will be indicated by your professor.

When citing references, APA style requires two things. First, in-text citations must be provided in the paper. For example:

According to Smith (2010), individuals are more likely to participate in shoplifting if they have friends who also shoplift, supporting social learning theory.

or

High school students who have friends who participate in shoplifting are also more likely to engage in this behavior (Smith, 2010).

This type of citation is appropriate if the information from a study has been summarized in your own words (the majority of the paper should be in your own words). However, there are times that you may want to use a quotation taken from the original material. In that case, it is important to note exactly where that information came from, as follows:

According to Brown (2011), "It is extremely difficult to predict what increases the likelihood of marijuana use among adolescents" (p. 201).

Any information cited in your paper has to be included in the reference list, which may also be referred to as the bibliography (it's usually the last page of the manuscript). On your references page, the first line of each entry should be flush left with all other lines indented. Authors are listed showing last name then first initial, and names should be placed in alphabetical order by the first author of each reference. Journal names should be listed in full, using all punctuation and capitalization as indicated. For example, a reference page may contain the following entries:

Benjamin, I. (2011). Girls are bullies too. *Journal of Aggression, 43*(2), 123–145.

Davis, Q., & Robertson, F. Writing can be easy for everyone! *English Language Composition, 13*(2), 5–10.

As noted earlier, it is important to consult the APA manual or website for a full list of appropriate methods to cite in your writing or in your references/bibliography page depending upon the source.

Plagiarism. Possibly the most important factor impacting the quality of any term paper is plagiarism. Plagiarism is the use of another person's ideas or words without giving them proper credit (i.e., without citing them correctly). Often done unintentionally by students, repercussions of this kind of technical mistake can earn you a zero on the assignment, a failing grade in the class, or even a hearing before your school's academic judicial board. A common method of plagiarism is directly copying and pasting text without placing it in quotations or summarizing it in your own words. Sneakier students may intentionally copy and paste shorter passages from sources to avoid detection, or even mix and match materials into text and claim it as their own.

Students are often not aware that turning in text from a paper that they have written for another class is plagiarism, unless both professors agree to its use. In other words, using your own words can also be considered cheating on an assignment. In addition, the overuse of someone else's materials or providing very little original work is considered plagiarism. Even if all the material in your text is properly cited, your term paper or essay must contain some of your own writing.

In order to avoid plagiarism, check with your professor or the writing center at your university to determine if you are citing materials properly. Writing centers are also excellent resources where undergraduates can work on basic to advanced writing skills and paper organization. Also, run your paper through TurnItIn (turnitin.com) or other plagiarism-checking websites (e.g., grammarly.com, paperrater.com, and others) to make sure you are giving credit appropriately. All academic institutions will have information posted online regarding what is considered plagiarism, and that information will usually include the school's policies with regard to punishment for those who violate the rules. Ten types of plagiarism are identified and discussed at http://www.turnitin.com/assets/en_us/media/plagiarism_spectrum.php.

Professional and Technical Writing Forms in Criminal Justice

Examples of these forms can be found in Appendix A.

It's All in the Details

Police Report Writing

Successful police work requires a lot of good writing. Police reports must be completed after criminal events and are often mandated by even relatively simple things such as a car accident. Police reports typically include (1) accounts of the event provided by individuals involved at the scene (offenders, victims, and witnesses); (2) a formal description of the event; and (3) a list of relevant items, or evidence. In addition, diagrams of an accident or crime scene may also be included. Police reports require a style of writing that is quite different from academic writing. These reports need to be written concisely and in everyday language (using first-person pronouns). When writing a police report, remember to do the following:

1. Use specific names (if possible) and pronouns. Rather than stating "victim 1" or "officer 3," use a person's name and refer to yourself as the officer writing the report as "I." *I interviewed the victim, Susan Jones.*

2. Each sentence or bullet point on the report should not include multiple concepts but rather have only one idea per sentence. *Susan Jones said that she was hit in the face by her boyfriend with his fist. Her boyfriend, Robert Smith, did not have any visible injuries.*

3. In addition, avoid making lists in a sentence and using many commas. *Inside Robert Smith's apartment, I found cocaine on the dining room table. I also found marijuana in the kitchen.*

4. Utilize specific descriptions of events, people, and places. For example, describe a person involved in a criminal event as specifically as possible, to include things such as hair color, eye color, height, and so on. The more specificity the better, as it leaves less room for questioning by defense attorneys.

5. Finally, use simple language. Remember, the information provided by the report could be used in court to help convict an offender, so you do not want to leave room for error or provide only vague statements. *The couple live together at #6 Westfield Apartments.*

While this form of writing may appear to be choppy, police reports are not meant to be essays. Instead, they are usually placed on a form that contains empty fields to be filled in with the information that is expected to be reported by an officer.

Get It All Down on Paper

Presentence Investigation Reports

Many criminal justice graduates will obtain employment in the fields of probation or parole and will be required to write extensively as a part of their job. One of the main requirements is the construction of the presentence investigation report, a document that provides the life history of an offender. This form contains information on an offender's criminal career, personal history, and professional experiences, to name a few items.

Presentence reports are written in third person and generally in essay format. So, the probation officer will refer to the offender by name and discuss in a narrative the information requested. Whereas some parts of the form require only short answers, other parts may need more thorough discussion. A presentence form is used by judges in deciding the appropriate sentence for an offender. When properly written, it allows judges to consider not only the current offense but also the life history of the offender and factors that may influence his or her potential for future criminality. The report should answer questions such as: Does the offender have a violent history? Was she a victim of abuse as a child? The judge may choose to provide a more punitive sentence than he would without having the information in the report, or the judge may order a sentence involving more rehabilitative programming.

Victim-Impact Statements

A victim-impact statement is made by an offender during court proceedings (often at the sentencing stage) to allow the victim to express his or her feelings about victimization and to describe the damage that an offender did. Victim-impact statements can be provided to the court in a variety of ways. Some courts will allow handwritten or typed notes by the victim that can be read by the victim or a victim-witness advocate. These types of statements are more open-ended and not too restrictive in terms of length or content. Other victim-impact statements are written onto a preexisting standardized form. When filling out such a form, a victim is asked a series of yes/no questions regarding the extent of physical and psychological injuries that he or she may have suffered. A few blanks may be on the form, allowing the victim to provide descriptions. Victims are also typically asked to provide information on the amount of financial losses in specific categories (i.e., the value of items stolen, lost wages from work, medical bills and associated expenses) so restitution can be calculated. Lastly, some courts may allow a victim to provide input with regard to his feelings about an appropriate sentence for the offender.

Discussion Questions _____

1. Explain why good writing skills are important in the field of criminal justice.

2. In your opinion, what is the most difficult part of writing a class paper?

3. Discuss how a professor or class assignment helped you to become a better writer.

7 Making Good Choices in the Social and Professional World

In Chapter 5, we discussed the importance of good communications when applying for jobs or internships. Once you have scored an interview, it is imperative to continue to maintain professional decorum online and offline. In fact, you should start developing a professional image long before you actually apply for any type of position. This chapter discusses different ways of meeting criminal justice stakeholders and the kinds of positive behaviors that ensure a successful job interview. In addition, we examine ways to proactively and retroactively clean up your personal and professional history to showcase the best "you" to potential employers.

Bring Your Best to an Interview

It's All in Who You Know

Do you have to know someone at an organization to become employed there? Absolutely not! However, networking is an extremely important part of preparing for employment after graduation. The criminal justice system is one of the largest employers in the nation, but yet it is an intimate community of interactive stakeholders who are often more than happy to share their opinions of others. In other words, getting your name out there in the justice community, and making a positive impression on everyone you meet, can be very helpful when trying to win a job over dozens of other applicants. There are a few ways you can be a proactive networker while still a student.

Attend career fairs at your university or college. Most institutions will have at least one career fair each year. Some of them are very large and organizations that attend represent multiple disciplines, whereas others are focused on specific fields (like probation, parole, and reentry). Either way, put on some nice clothes and stop by the career fair. Introduce yourself and indicate your interests to representatives of organizations and agencies that attend, and ask them questions. Offer potential employers a copy of your fantastic résumé (that you created a few chapters ago). Résumés allow organizational representatives to put a face with a name, as well as to remember how intriguing and professional you were at the fair.

Volunteer. You cannot just show up at the local branch of the Federal Bureau of Investigation and volunteer to help with their work. However, you can participate in extracurricular activities that allow you to meet people working in the field of criminal justice. For instance, volunteering to participate at a local elementary school during a safety fair will give you the opportunity to meet important justice stakeholders. Likewise, universities often have educational fairs on sexual assault, dating safety, and drinking behaviors that involve law enforcement and victim services. Volunteering to participate and work at a booth is also a positive networking opportunity.

Attend criminal justice conferences. Academics in the criminal justice field annually attend conferences to present research, develop new projects, and meet others with similar interests. In addition, such conferences provide opportunities to meet scholars and practitioners and to attend social events where everyone gathers. The American Society of Criminology (ASC), for example, meets every November, and the Academy of Criminal Justice Sciences (ACJS) meets in March every year. ACJS generally attracts more practitioners (i.e., those working in law enforcement, corrections, victims' services), whereas ASC attendees tend to be more academic in their focus. In addition to these large national meetings, there are regional conferences every year, as well as meetings of the American Correctional Association and the American Probation and Parole Association, to name but a few. Attend any of these meetings and you will have the opportunity to explore your fields of interests, meet active members of the justice community, and ask questions. In addition, joining these organizations demonstrates an interest in the criminal justice field and is a great résumé builder. Student membership rates are very affordable, and regional organizations are generally affordable for students to join. For example, the Southern Criminal Justice Association charges only $15 for a year-long student membership.

Take a few minutes to complete Worksheet 7.1 (page 75). Doing so may help you focus on the steps you need to take to pursue your ideal career goal.

Represent Yourself Well

Maneuvering the Job Interview Process

From the instant you receive a call asking if you would like to interview, until the last time you communicate with a potential employer, it is important to put your most professional "you" in the limelight. This does *not* mean acting like someone you are not or lying about your credentials. It *does* mean presenting yourself in the most favorable way possible. This section discusses important steps to ensuring the best possible interview.

First, *be polite to everyone you encounter.* Whether it is a company administrator who is interviewing you or the janitor who greets you in the hallway, always be polite. Greet people sincerely, offer a handshake in appropriate situations, and express your gratitude for the consideration given you. If the receptionist offers you something to drink or directions to the meeting room, thank him or her for their assistance. Why is this important? Because everyone deserves respect no matter their position, and you never know who is going to bend the ear of the personnel manager or company CEO about your manners—whether good or bad!

Second, *be flexible and accommodating.* It can be difficult to coordinate a time for an interview if both parties have inflexible schedules. Since you are the one who is trying to get a job, try to be as flexible as possible when scheduling appointments and calls. For instance, if the human resources manager asks about your availability for interviews or paperwork completion, do not provide only one day and time. Indicate several days and times that would work for you, indicating your interest in the position and your availability to work with others.

Next, *be an expert on yourself.* One of the worst things a person can do in an interview is appear to be disorganized and aloof. Take time to carefully review your résumé and any other information that you have provided about yourself. In other words, make an effort to understand how you look to others. If the hiring manager asks you a question about a line on your résumé and you don't remember it, your verbal and nonverbal cues may seem to indicate that you were lying when you prepared the résumé or that you are not prepared for the interview.

Dress for success. Not every job interview requires a suit and tie or dress. You can determine what apparel is correct for an interview by reviewing the position. For instance, an interview for assistant district attorney equates to business professional clothing (suit and tie), but an intern at the local police department could wear nice slacks and a button-up shirt. However, there are some basic rules of thumb for every interview that will allow you to present yourself at your best.

1. Wear conservative clothing. This does not mean you cannot be fashionable and contemporary, but for women it means *not* wearing a low-cut blouse, short skirt, or tank top. For men, jeans and a T-shirt are not good choices for a job interview. Avoid flashy, sheer, or ill-fitting clothing, and make sure your clothes match.

2. Appear neat and clean. That "just rolled out of bed look" is never good for a job interview. Wash your clothes before wearing them, and use that fancy piece of equipment in your apartment (the iron!) to get all the wrinkles out. You do not have to spend a lot of money on an interview outfit, but you should look like you put effort into getting prepared for the occasion. In addition, shower, shave, fix your hair, and wear deodorant. Are you laughing? You would be amazed how many people do not follow these simple rules.

3. Date night apparel should be kept for date night. Wearing flashy clothing with lots of accessories, bright and heavy jewelry, and super-long fingernails does not convey a professional look. There should be no question that you are prepared for the interview, and not going to a club.

4. Cover up the tattoos. Tattoo owners are proud of their tats, as they usually have a special meaning for them. That's fine! However, body art are can be extremely distracting to an employer when he or she is trying to assess your qualifications for a job. If your arms

are covered in tattoos, wear long sleeves. Facial piercings, with the exception of earrings, should be removed. Keep in mind that the person interviewing you sees you as potentially representing the organization, and a huge nose barbell may not be the image they want others to see.

Prepare for the inevitable. Especially with entry-level positions, interviewers will inevitably ask many of the same questions. Rather than being caught off guard, have answers that show you've put some time into thinking about the answers. The following questions are common interview questions:

1. Why did your apply for this job?

2. What makes you qualified for this position?

3. What are your strengths? Weaknesses?

4. Where do you see yourself in 5 years?

5. Tell me about a time you had a conflict with a coworker and how you dealt with it.

Also, it would benefit you to know about the organization before your interview. Knowledge of its mission, the number of employees, and other such information would show you are interested in the position and the agency, not just a paycheck.

Seal the deal. Once the interview is complete and you have left the building, the first item of business is to send a thank-you note to the interviewer. This can be done via e-mail or regular mail, but it is imperative you thank a person for her time. This simple act can make the difference between a job offer and a job rejection.

Keep your mouth shut. This may be the most important rule of all! No matter where you interview, remember the criminal justice world is a small community. It is a guarantee that the person who interviewed you knows someone else in the criminal justice community who knows someone else who . . . well, you get the picture. So, if you do not get the job and post on your Facebook page that the interviewer was stupid and ugly, or you call your friend and tell him the interviewer was an idiot, don't assume it will never get back to that person. That interviewer may have told another friend what a great candidate you were and suggest offering an alternative position to you. Your mother was right: If you have nothing nice to say, do not say anything at all.

Think about the characteristics that describe a professional, and complete Worksheet 7.2 (page 76).

Universities and colleges have some form of a career services office to help students prepare for all facets of employment. These offices offer assistance in résumé and cover letter preparation, job interview practice, and other helpful hints to succeed in the job market. Better yet, employment opportunities and job advertisements are available in these offices—so go check them out!

Be Who You Want to Be Online

So Much Cooler Online . . .

As one country music superstar so correctly put it, you are so much cooler online. When you are online, you can be whoever you want to be and portray whatever image you like. But if you want to present an outlandish self or outrageous ideas, then it's best to post anonymously or with a pseudonym. Let's face it: Most of us become a little more narcissistic (or a *lot* more narcissistic) during social networking. The frequency of "selfie" posting has increased so dramatically that we can actually buy a stick to take our own photo anywhere, anytime, even with no one around to take our picture. So, post as many pictures of yourself and your cat as you like . . . as long as it doesn't cost you a job.

The majority of Americans have become very Internet dependent, if not addicted. How many people do you see walking around with their heads down, buried in a smartphone? With all the convenience we have as consumers, remember that potential employers also have the ability to view social networking websites. Checking out a person on Google and looking at Facebook or Instagram pages have become a routine part of the review process used by many organizations to assess a potential employee. Even if they don't surf the Web themselves, employers have the freedom to find out what they want about you with a simple click by using third parties who compile and sell background information. So think about all of the posts, pictures, and information that are associated with yourself online. What would they say about you to an employer? Would the Federal Bureau of Investigation want to hire a person with anti-government posts or personal images of nonstop drunken behavior? Would your county clerk office want to hire someone who is scantily dressed and making obscene gestures and sexual innuendos online?

There are two ways to adapt your online presence so that potential employers will see you in a positive light. First, take a retroactive approach. In other words, review all of your posts, pictures, and statements associated with your social networking pages. Then ask yourself: Would you want someone conservative (like your grandmother) to view those posts? If the answer is no, removing the posts is in your best interest. Second, take a proactive approach from now on with your life. Refrain from consistent negative commentary, including discriminatory jokes and gossip. Do not post pictures of yourself in compromising situations.

Unfortunately, individuals entering the job market today face the issue of having intimate aspects of their lives revealed online. Of course, all of us have done embarrassing, crazy, silly, and even illegal things. Previous to the emergence of the Internet for personal use, we never had to worry about our mistakes being posted on the Internet for all to see.

Staying on the Right Side of the Law

As a criminal justice major, you are more than aware of the importance of adhering to the law. It is especially important for you to avoid legal trouble because you plan to work in a field that is intimately associated with enforcing the law. Unfortunately, some criminal justice majors find themselves charged, prosecuted, and convicted of criminal offenses. Often, these impulsive behaviors result in a lifetime of repercussions.

A common criminal charge against students is driving under the influence (DUI) or driving while intoxicated (DWI). Conviction of a DUI or DWI charge can result in a suspended license or loss of automobile insurance, which limits your ability to reach a job site. Some employers have mandatory firing policies for employees who receive a DUI or DWI, especially felony DUIs and DWIs. Having a conviction may also prevent you from obtaining a job interview. Institutions of higher education sometimes have the option of denying you admission because of a criminal conviction, or they may deny federal aid to pay for your tuition. However, the most important consideration is for individuals who want to pursue a career in law enforcement. A felony conviction will automatically disqualify you from working as a police officer—even if it occurred years ago.

Drug use and underage drinking are other common charges that a number of college students face. These charges may limit career opportunities in the law enforcement area. Some law enforcement agencies will excuse drug convictions (especially if they happened long ago and especially if they involved small amounts of certain drugs) or misdemeanor charges. However, other agencies refuse any applicant with a history of drug use or conviction. Keep in mind that most of the time, the law enforcement screening process involves a polygraph, and admission of drug use can disqualify a person from employment. Lying about your past drug use is not advisable as the professional repercussions can be even more detrimental than telling the truth. If you have an arrest or conviction on your record, be forthright about it!

Lastly, maintaining a good overall driving record and a good credit rating is important to all employers. Law enforcement employers are especially looking for candidates who do not have speeding tickets, unpaid parking tickets, or other driving-related offenses. In addition, candidates who have good credit ratings and no collections issues are viewed as responsible candidates for positions (especially if the management of money is involved).

The best advice we can give is to be aware of the requirements and restrictions of criminal justice jobs. If you have a desire to be a federal law enforcement agent, cease any marijuana or other illicit drug use immediately. Corrections officers must not have an incarceration record. Many graduating students are dismayed when they apply for a job and are denied employment based on a past mistake. Remember, this field is all about upholding the law, so candidates who appear to be unethical and who do not seem to have respect for the law will not be considered. Criminal justice academic and practitioner organizations all have a Code of Ethics for their members, which is another indication that representing and upholding community values and morals is very important.

Conclusion

There's an old saying: "Birds of a feather flock together." College can be a fun time for everyone, but it is imperative to keep in mind that late-night parties and crazy antics are short-lived. Some of your friends may not have as much to lose as you if involvement in fun goes too far. Keep this in mind when making decisions about what you do and who you spend your time with.

Discussion Questions

1. Is there anything in your current social networking profile that you believe does NOT reflect positive qualities as a potential employee? If so, what can you do about it?

2. Can a person have a lot of body art and still be considered professional? Why or why not?

3. Consider a past behavior that could have or did affect your employment opportunities. What would you have done differently?

WORKSHEET 7.1

What Do I Want to Be When I Grow Up?

1. What is my ideal job? _____

2. What are the qualifications for this position?

    a. _____

    b. _____

    c. _____

3. What can I start doing to prepare for this position?

    a. _____

    b. _____

    c. _____

4. Are there classes that I can take in my program of study to prepare for this position?

    a. _____

    b. _____

    c. _____

5. Does a foreign language help my chances of obtaining this position?

WORKSHEET 7.2

Are You Professional?

List three characteristics of a person you would view as professional.

1.

2.

3.

Do any of these characteristics reflect your current persona?

Do any of these characteristics reflect those of your professor?

Do any of your friends have these characteristics?

8
Criminal Justice Internships and Service-Learning Opportunities

The benefit of pursuing a degree in higher education is you are able to learn about diverse topics, attitudes, and values on a local and global scale. Criminal justice professionals encounter diverse populations on a daily basis, so it is important to have this knowledge before jumping into a career. However, it is the hope of all educators that students are able to expand their learning outside the classroom walls and experience the reality of the daily life of criminal justice professionals. Two methods of gaining real-world experience, while also earning academic credit, are internships and service learning. This chapter explores the main components of each of these learning methodologies.

Objectives of an Internship

The benefit of going shopping is the ability to try out an item before the big step of taking ownership. Whether it is a pair of shoes, a couch, or a car, an individual can figure out what works best for him by trying something on and taking it out for a spin! The same goes for experimenting with a new career, and the average person changes her career several times before settling into a field. Participating in an internship during undergraduate or graduate school allows a student to better decide if a particular field is the right fit.

A student participating in an internship will reap many benefits from the experience. Most importantly, first-hand knowledge of the operations of a criminal justice agency will be gained. Interns will understand the daily operations of an agency, the contribution to the community, and the community reaction to the responsibilities of an agency. In addition, realities will dispel myths commonly held about the agency. For example, criminal justice students often assume that police officers are constantly breaking down doors and investigating homicides (common to what is portrayed on television shows). While police work can be extremely dangerous, as well as exciting, there are several other components to the responsibilities of an officer. An internship with a law enforcement agency is usually an eye-opening experience, either fueling the passion for the job or encouraging an intern to explore other careers.

Another benefit of an internship is developing skills and knowledge of a particular career, as well as applying current understanding based on course content from a program of study and life experience. Generally, interns spend an intensive duration of time with an agency and get to learn many facets of a particular career. Often, they get to participate in certain activities or at least be a spectator during activities such as investigations or court proceedings. The knowledge interns have accumulated in their classes can be applied. In other words, students can have that moment of "Wow, I learned that in class!" or "Hey, my professor was right about that!"

Lastly, an internship can allow for internal reflection. By watching an agency's employees in action for multiple weeks, an intern can gain an appreciation for the physical and emotional stress associated with the position. Conversely, an intern can see the value of the services provided and the reward associated with helping others. Interns can also reflect on their own personal beliefs and values in order to analyze if they would "fit in" with a particular agency. For instance, individuals who support a more rehabilitative stance in regard to corrections are more suited to employment at a drug court or treatment facility, rather than a corrections officer in a more punitive prison.

Once an intern has become immersed in an agency, it is the expectation that he will become socialized with the other employees. He will learn the appropriate dress for the job, learn behaviors that are expected and accepted, and hopefully form collegial relationships with other employees. While the majority of internships are not paid as a real job, the intention is to give the intern the complete experience of the job.

See the example of a criminal justice internship application at the end of this chapter (Worksheet 8.1, page 82).

Components of an Internship

It is important to keep in mind that every university and college has different requirements in regard to graduating with a criminal justice–related degree. Some institutions of higher learning require an internship in order to graduate, while others allow it as an elective option. Other

Am I on the Right Track?

institutions, especially those featuring degrees earned solely online, are less likely to offer an internship option.

At institutions that offer the internship option, there is a faculty or staff member who serves as an *internship coordinator*. Some universities will employ one full-time person who is responsible for all internships, and other universities will assign a certain number of interns to a few faculty members. This coordinator, or manager, is responsible for making sure the intern completes all academic components of the internship, as well as professional requirements. Internship coordinators can help a student find an internship or, at the very least, approve the contract of terms between the agency and intern. The internship coordinator handles any issues of inappropriate behavior on the end of the intern, or the agency for that matter. Internship coordinators will sometimes perform site visits of the agency to allow the intern to demonstrate internship responsibilities, meet with the supervisor of the intern, and get a tour of the facility.

Internships have *professional requirements*, in other words, duties expected of the intern while at the agency. Interns working at a defense attorney's office will most likely perform filing duties, make deliveries, and potentially assist with evidence during court. Interns at a sheriff's office may have the opportunity to go on ride-alongs and watch other law enforcement functions. Either way, in order to complete the professional requirements of an internship, an intern must perform a required number of *service hours*. If the internship lasts an entire semester, it is not unusual for the intern to be required to work 30 to 40 hours per week for the 15-week semester (450 to 600 hours for the semester). Keep in mind, the majority of internships are unpaid, but this qualifies as 12 hours of academic credit, which is equal to a full load of classes. Other internships that require fewer service hours equate to fewer academic credits, such as 3 to 9 hours of academic credit.

Keep in mind that in order to earn academic credit, interns must also complete academic work. Obviously this is dependent upon the program, but this can be accomplished in a few different ways. Internships that last an entire semester may require a weekly report to the coordinator regarding the duties of the intern and application of knowledge from courses. Midterm papers and final papers are often required, as well as an assessment of the entire internship experience. Lastly, the internship supervisor is asked to complete evaluations of the intern (see Worksheet 8.2, page 84). A final grade on the A to F scale, or sometimes Satisfactory or Unsatisfactory, is given the intern at the completion of the semester.

Objectives of Service Learning

Another option for applying knowledge from the classroom to real-life experiences is a service-learning course. Service-learning courses involve projects outside the classroom that address community needs, in addition to academic work that involves reflection of the concepts used. For instance, a service-learning course on the broken windows theory would involve performing community service activities to clean up a dilapidated community (painting over graffiti, planting flowers, etc.), as well as discussion about the theoretical background of broken windows and discussing its policy implications. Service-learning courses involve both volunteering via the fieldwork process and earning academic credit for the service.

Advocates of service learning insist that the process must be approached with a reciprocity focus. In other words, there should not be a one-sided beneficiary. The students in one of these courses should be serving the community, but they also receive a benefit from participating in the process. This benefit is not financial; rather, it is the satisfaction of helping others and understanding the purpose of the work.

The focus of a service-learning course can depend upon the type of institution sponsoring the course. Large universities require their faculty members to be more research focused, so it is unlikely there will be support for smaller community projects. However, service-learning courses with a global focus that can also integrate the faculty member's research is a positive alternative. Many liberal arts colleges focus on social justice issues and encourage work in the community. Women's colleges and historically black universities might also focus on projects that meet the needs of their communities.

Components of Service-Learning Coursework

A service-learning class must be academically rigorous in order to be counted as academic credit. Students are required to complete multiple academic components in addition to the community service activities.

Generally, the basic components of any course, such as *exams and quizzes,* also exist in service-learning classes. However, an important part of service-learning classes is maintaining a *journal.* Students record their activities of the week, reflections of the process, and analysis of its impact.

Students are also required to complete a *project* of some type in service-learning classes, often in a group setting. This can entail completion of a community-service project, development of a workshop or educational program, or involvement in a mentoring program. No matter the project, students are required to document the entire project development process, assess its strengths and weaknesses, and discuss its applicability to a real-world setting. Some examples of service-learning projects that could be applied in the criminal justice field are the following:

- Creation of a neighborhood watch program in a community
- Development of a police officer mentoring program at an elementary school
- Implementation of a community park cleanup in a high-crime neighborhood
- Assisting a victim-advocacy organization in the initiation of a safety fair at a local university

An important factor to consider with a service-learning class is the number of *service hours* required for completion. In other words, how many hours must a student dedicate to work in the community and complete the assigned project? The professor will provide due dates of academic requirements, as well as community project requirements. Often, much like an internship, a contract or partnership agreement between a community agency and the student is signed that outlines the service agreement between the student and agency. This document will indicate the number of hours the student agrees to work for the agency, as well as the tasks that will be completed.

Discussion Questions

1. Students are often uninterested in doing an internship (if it isn't required) because most internship work is unpaid. What might you say to encourage a fellow student to apply for an internship?

2. Which courses in criminal justice do you believe could incorporate a service-learning component, and why?

WORKSHEET 8.1

Example of a Criminal Justice Internship Application

Last_____ First_____Middle_____

Internship Semester: Fall_____ Spring_____ Summer_____ Year: 20_____

Personal Information

1. ID: _____

2. Current School Address (address where you receive mail):

    _____

    _____

3. City: _____ State: _____ Zip: _____

4. Phone number where you can be reached: _____

5. Cell: _____

6. E-Mail Address: _____

7. Other E-Mail Address: _____

8. Permanent Address:

    _____

    _____

9. City_____ State:_____ Zip:_____

10. Permanent Phone: _____

11. Driver's License Number: _____ State Issued: _____

Academic Information

Grade Point Average: _____ GPA in Major: _____

Semester Hours Completed: _____

List Academic Honors, Scholarships, Fellowships, etc.:

_____

_____

_____

_____

Extra-Curricular Activities:

_____

_____

_____

_____

Internship Information

Which area(s) of criminal justice are you interested in doing your internship?

_____ Police Department _____ Sheriff Office _____ Agency of the Courts
_____ Federal Law Enforcement _____ State Law Enforcement

State any career goals or plans you may have.

_____ Criminal Law (Prosecution or Defense) _____ Probation (Community Corrections)
_____ Adult Corrections _____ Private Security

_____
_____
_____
_____

Briefly explain any experiences, special training, or academic background that you feel would qualify you for a particular internship in criminal justice.

_____
_____
_____
_____

Special Skills, Talents, etc.

_____
_____
_____
_____

List any impairments (physical, mental, or medical) that might disqualify you from certain internships.

_____
_____
_____
_____

Explain anything in your background that might disqualify you from certain internships (drug/alcohol usage, credit problems, criminal charges or convictions, excessive infractions, etc.).

_____
_____
_____
_____

I certify that to the best of my knowledge and belief, the above statements are true and hereby authorize representatives of the State of _____ to verify any information given above. I hereby authorize the issuance of my official transcript to representatives of the State of _____. Furthermore, I authorize representatives of the State of _____ to respond to any reference requests with true and complete information relevant to my application or my suitability for any internship for which I have applied.

Date: _____ Signature: _____

No application will be considered unless accompanied by student copy of your transcript.

WORKSHEET 8.2

Example of an Internship Agency Supervisor Evaluation of Student

Student Name: _____   Date: _____

Internship Agency: _____

Supervisor: _____

Please rate the student from a 1 to 4, with 1 being poor performance and 4 being excellent performance.

Adherence to professional demeanor	1	2	3	4
Adherence to professional dress	1	2	3	4
Punctuality	1	2	3	4
Ability to follow instructions	1	2	3	4
Ability to work independently	1	2	3	4
Ability to work as a team member	1	2	3	4
Ability to interact professionally with clients	1	2	3	4
Ability to interact professionally with staff	1	2	3	4
Respectfulness toward diverse populations	1	2	3	4

OVERALL RATING:

Appendix _____

GOVERNMENT REPORT 1

OFFENSE/INCIDENT REPORT

INSTRUCTIONS ARE PRINTED SEPARATELY. IF ADDITIONAL SPACE IS NEEDED, USE REVERSE OF FORM; IDENTIFY ITEMS.

1. TYPE
- ☐ a. ORIGINAL
- ☐ b. CONTINUATION
- ☐ c. SUPPLEMENT OR FOLLOWUP

2. CODE NO.	2a. SORT	3. TYPE OF OFFENSE OR INCIDENT	4. CASE CONTROL NUMBER

5. BUILDING NUMBER	6. ADDRESS

7. NAME OF AGENCY/BUREAU	8. AGENCY/BUREAU CODE	9. SPECIFIC LOCATION	10. LOCATION CODE

11a. DATE OF OFFENSE/INCIDENT	11a. TIME OF OFFENSE/INCIDENT	12. DAY	13a. DATE REPORTED	13b. TIME REPORTED	14. DAY

15. JURISDICTION (X)
☐ EXCLUSIVE ☐ CONCURRENT ☐ PARTIAL ☐ PROPRIETARY

16. NO. OF DEMONSTRATORS	17. NO. EVACUATED	a. TIME START	b. TIME END

18. PERSONS INVOLVED

ID CODE (a)	NAME AND ADDRESS (b)	AGE (c)	SEX (d)	RACE (e)	INJURY CODE (f)	TELEPHONE (g)
	Last Name, First, Middle Initial					HOME
	Number, Street, Apt. No., City and State					BUSINESS
	Last Name, First, Middle Initial					HOME
	Number, Street, Apt. No., City and State					BUSINESS

19. VEHICLE

a. STATUS	b. YEAR	c. MAKE	d. MODEL	e. COLOR *(Top/Bottom)*	f. IDENTIFYING CHARACTERISTICS

STOLEN	SUSPECT	g. REGIS- TRATION ▶	YEAR	STATE	TAG NO.	h. VIN	i. VALUE
GOV''T	PERSONAL						
VANDALIZED	RECOVERED						

20. ITEMS TAKEN

a. NAME OF ITEM	b. QUANTITY	c. OWNERSHIP ☐ GOV'T ☐ PERSONAL	d. BRAND NAME

e. SERIAL NO.	f. COLOR	g. MODEL

h. VALUE	i. UNUSUAL OR UNIQUE FEATURES

j. PROPERTY WAS ☐ SECURRED ☐ UNSECURED	k. STATUS OF PROPERTY ☐ RECOVERED ☐ MISSING ☐ PARTIAL RECOVERY	VALUE RECOVERED

l. NAME OF ITEM	m. QUANTITY	n. OWNERSHIP ☐ GOV'T ☐ PERSONAL	o. BRAND NAME

p. SERIAL NO.	q. COLOR	r. MODEL

s. VALUE	t. UNUSUAL OR UNIQUE FEATURES

u. PROPERTY WAS ☐ SECURRED ☐ UNSECURED	v. STATUS OF PROPERTY ☐ RECOVERED ☐ MISSING ☐ PARTIAL RECOVERY	VALUE RECOVERED

21. NARRATIVE *(If additional space is needed, use blank sheet and attach.)*

22. NOTIFICATION	TIME		23a. EVIDENCE ☐ YES ☐ NO	23b. TAG NO.	23c. TYPE
	NOTIFIED	ARRIVED			
a. Other Police Agency			23d. WHERE STORED		

24. ATTACHMENTS (Mark "X" where applicable)		
a. CONTINUATION SHEET	d. STATEMENT(S)	
b. GSA FORM 3157		
c. PROPERTY RECEIPT(S)	e. SUPPLEMENTAL	
f. OTHER ATTACHMENTS (Specify)		

(22 continued)

- b. Fire Department
- c. Ambulance
- d. Building Manager
- e. OTHER (Specify)

25. SUSPECT STATUS		26. DISPOSITION OF SUSPECT	
a. NOT IDENTIFIED		a. ARRESTED	b. NOT ARRESTED
b. GOVERNMENT EMPLOYEE		c. RELEASED	d. N/A
c. GOVERNMENT CONTRACT			CITATION NUMBER
d. NON-GOVERNMENT EMPLOYEE		d. CITATION ISSUED ▶	
e. N/A			

NOTE: Complete GSA Form 3157 where this is a Suspect, Att. Burglary, Burglary, Att. Robbery, Robbery, or a Weapon is used.

27. TIME			28. REVIEWED BY		
a. RECEIVED	b. ARRIVED	a. TYPE ☐ FPS	b. SIGNATURE		d. DATE
c. RETURNED TO SERVICE		☐ GG	c. NAME (Printed)		

29a. BADGE	29b. NAME (Printed)	29c. SIGNATURE	29d. DATE

30. CASE REFERRED TO			31. CASE	32. APPROVING OFFICIAL	
a. FPS DETECTIVE	b. LOCAL POLICE	c. STATE POLICE		a. SIGNATURE	b. DATE
d. FBI	e. IG	f. N/A	a. OPEN		
g. OTHER (Specify)			b. CLOSED	c. NAME (Printed)	
			c. UNFOUNDED		

33. DETECTIVE STATUS				
a. CASE NUMBER	b. HOW CLOSED ☐ INACTIVE ☐ ARREST ☐ OTHER MEANS	c. SUSPECT ☐ DEVELOPED ☐ ARRESTED	d. ENTERED NCIC ☐ YES ☐ NO ☐ N/A	
☐ e. PROPERTY RECOVERED	f. VALUE OF PROPERTY	g. CLEARED NCIC ☐ YES ☐ NO ☐ N/A	h. REFERRED TO	
			i. DATE REFERRAL ACCEPTED	

21. NARRATIVE (If additional space is needed, use blank sheet and attach.)

GOVERNMENT REPORT 2

UNITED STATES v. _____

COURT DOCKET NUMBER _____

INDIVIDUAL VICTIM IMPACT STATEMENT/FINANCIAL CRIME

How have you and members of your family been affected by this crime?
Please continue this statement on an additional sheet of paper if you wish.

Have you or members of your family received counseling as a result of this crime?
Please explain.

Have you filed a civil suit against the defendant? If yes, please list the case name, court location, and docket number.

VICTIM IMPACT STATEMENT/FINANCIAL CRIME

Do you relate to people differently since the crime? Please explain.

How has the crimes affected you and your family's lifestyle? Please explain.

Has the crime affected your family's livelihood? Please explain.

Have you experienced any of the following reactions to the crime: PLEASE REALIZE THESE ARE NORMAL REACTIONS TO A TRAUMATIC EVENT OR SITUATION.

Anger   Anxiety   Fear   Grief   Guilt   Sleep Loss   Nightmares
Appetite Change   Trouble Concentrating   Repeated Memory of Crime

Please describe any other reactions to the crime committed.
Numb   Chronic Fatigue   Unsafe   Uncontrolled Crying   Depression

Do you feel the defendant is or will be a threat to you, your family, or the community?
Yes No, Please explain.

VICTIM IMPACT STATEMENT/FINANCIAL CRIME

What else would you like the Judge to know about the defendant, or your situation as a result of the crime?

If a victim consents, the Court may also make restitution in services in lieu of money, or make restitution to a person or organization designated by a victim. If you are interested in this option, please explain.

1. Please list your actual financial losses from this crime. List only those items for which you have not been or do not expect to be repaid. Please attach receipts or other records whenever possible. (Use additional paper if needed.) Please differentiate any monies already repaid by a defendant.

2. Have you been assessed any additional taxes, penalties or interest by the federal government as a result of this case? If yes, please explain.

3. Have you or anyone on your behalf initiated civil action against any party as a result of this offense? If yes, please state the case name, docket number and court of jurisdiction.

VICTIM IMPACT STATEMENT/FINANCIAL CRIME

4. If you have suffered any other expenses as a result of this crime, please list them on an additional sheet of paper. Include such items as counseling, medical bills, lost income and necessary child care, transportation, and other expenses related to participation in the investigation or prosecution of the offense or attendance at proceedings related to the offense. Please be specific and attach copies of receipts if possible.

Date:

Signature:

Printed Name:

CONFIDENTIAL

United States v. Case Number:

The address and telephone contact information provided below will only be provided to the presentence probation officer, and the United States Attorney's Office, unless a court order signed by the Judge authorizes the release of this page to the Court and attorney for the defendant.

Printed Name:

Signature:

Address:

Phone: (hm)   (wk)

Fax: E-Mail:

Index